MORALITY AND PUBLIC POLICY

Clem Henricson

D1615514

First published in Great Britain in 2016 by

Policy Press
University of Bristol
1-9 Old Park Hill
Bristol
BS2 8BB
UK
t: +44 (0)117 954 5940
pp-info@bristol.ac.uk
www.policypress.co.uk

North America office:
Policy Press
c/o The University of Chicago Press
1427 East 60th Street
Chicago, IL 60637, USA
t: +1 773 702 7700
f: +1 773 702 9756
sales@press.uchicago.edu
www.press.uchicago.edu

British Library Cataloguing in Publication Data
A catalogue record for this book is available from the British Library

Library of Congress Cataloging-in-Publication Data
A catalog record for this book has been requested

ISBN 978 1 44732 381 5 hardcover
ISBN 978 1 44732 382 2 paperback
ISBN 978 1 44732 385 3 ePub
ISBN 978 1 44732 386 0 Mobi

Cover design by David Rodgers
Front cover image: www.alamy.com
Printed and bound in Great Britain by CMP, Poole
Policy Press uses environmentally responsible print partners

Contents

Acknowledgements

As with any book from narrative to poetry to scientific interpretation – the influences are so broad and diffuse that it is impossible to do them justice in any attempt at acknowledgement. But for the record, I have learnt about the defects of a public policy system that fights shy of embracing the reality of morality from those who have engaged and striven with moral causes, who have exhibited commitment and ceaseless crusading. My thoughts have been moulded by the determination of these stalwarts who have made some headway against oppressive, out of date policies consequent on stasis at the morality–public policy interface. It is the hope of lessening the unnecessary burden on those seeking change and a better match between morality and policy that has prompted me to pen this think piece. It is a hope that public policy can better accommodate the moral dimension associated with changing social mores, personal relationships, matters of life and death and even welfare and finance. From modes of policing and criminal justice to equalities to family policy and human rights, I have been influenced by a striving for change that has cried out to be better facilitated by institutions of state and public administration.

For the development and refinement of the book itself I owe a particular debt of gratitude to Professor Alan Deacon, Dr Fatima Husain, Professor Kimmo Jokinen, Professor Ilan Katz, Professor Margaret O'Brien, Matthew Taylor and David Utting who generously gave of their expertise and insights from the conception of the book through to its fruition. And in particular I should like to thank those at Policy Press – Emily Watt, Laura Greaves, Susannah Emery and Rebecca Megson – who have supported this endeavour throughout; I could not have managed without their very great skill, commitment and patience.

Preface

Have you ever wondered why the moral sphere is segregated from core public policy? Why in the gestation of policy is morality hived off as the provenance of private conscience and the clerisy? We have separate development with the relegation of moral issues to some zone outside the mainstream of governmental concerns. Are governments too cowardly or ill equipped to address these matters? Certainly deficiency of intent and purpose springs to mind; it emphatically should not take so long for legislation to keep up with changes in social mores – changes in attitudes to matters such as assisted dying, abortion, homosexuality and cohabitation. Why does government hide behind the private member's bill, judicial rulings, loud protracted campaigns and flouting of the law that are so often the necessary prelude to change? Why is government dilatory and evasive, instead of embracing the essence of human relations – handling fluctuations and tensions head on? And what about the stuff of political governance – finance and welfare – why is an illusory dividing line drawn between these aspects of public policy and conventional 'morality' – why is private conscience accorded to the latter, but not the former in the face of party whipping?

There is, too, a collective anxiety at the policy morality interface induced by the perpetual moralistic incantation of 'never again'. 'Never again' we say in the full knowledge at a certain level of consciousness that, from negligence to sadism, it will be done again across institutions from finance, caring, criminal justice through to family life and individual relationships. We appear to have difficulty in acknowledging the true dimensions of the human condition and our failure to do so is hampering the development of a realistic pre-emptive public policy.

As a public policy analyst I have been beset by these doubts about the morality and public policy axis; the tensions need flushing out. There is also the context of the increasing prominence of morality in public discourse in the wake of a growing secular religious divide and enhanced scientific understanding of human behavioural dispositions. The gnawing doubts and their context constitute a heady brew – a brew that has been sufficient to prompt me to write this polemical think piece with the intention of stimulating a national debate on the precarious, flawed relationship between morality and public policy.

Clem Henricson
November 2015

ONE

Introduction:
why we need a better connection
between morality and public policy

For a materialist largely secular society the surge in public statements concerning morality has been surprisingly loud in the early 21st century. Contentious positioning can be witnessed not only in relation to condoning or opposing specific behaviours, but also in terms of analysing and pronouncing on the causes and functions that underpin morality. The latter dimension, the derivation and purpose of morality, has had a potent fillip as a consequence of concerns over a dwindling spirituality. Added grist to the mill has been the crusade to put a final nail in the coffin of God and metaphysical beliefs by Dawkins and others. There are quests to reinstate the significance of a spiritual dimension to life in a godless world ranging from atheistic Sunday assemblies, creaming the celebratory and moralistic aspects of religion, to the institution of fundamentalist beliefs and behaviours across the faith spectrum.

As potent as these multiple oppositional trends around the issue of spirituality have been, we have also witnessed scientific investigations into the operation of the brain and instincts that have had a significant impact on public debate. Darwin's (1871) identification of the social and other instincts has been revisited following the deciphering of the functions and intricacies of the brain. One could almost hear the collective sigh of relief, certainly within the secular lobby, as empathy, the pathway to pro-social behaviour, found a locus in verifiable physical matter (Singer and Lamm, 2009; Zaki and Ochsner, 2012). But contrary to expectations, the imperative to agonise through the tortuous corridors of concept and reasoning in moral philosophy has not receded. There has been much picking and choosing as to which parts of the brain, which impulses to promote in a process of ceaseless human imaging. For some, the majority perhaps, empathy has been chosen as the star human trait and feature of the brain meriting emphasis at the cost of giving a host of other impulses due recognition. Some philosophers, such as Mary Midgley in *Are you an Illusion?* (2014), query an over reliance on scientific interpretations of the brain. There are limitations as to how much we know as unquestionable truths.

And preferences and interpretations are still with us; it is apparent that whatever certainties may emerge, the way in which knowledge about human behaviour is interpreted and applied to social relations will remain a live question.

While recent treatises on the derivation of morality abound, they tend to be fragmentary expounding particular features rather than offering an overview of the causes, influences, impact and management of morality in a multicultural, fast changing society. Thus for example Greene in *Moral Tribes: Emotion, Reason and the Gap between Us and Them* (2014) offers a synthesis of neuroscience, psychology and philosophy, but does not relate these issues to public policy. Rose and Abi-Rached in *Neuro: The New Brain Sciences and the Management of the Mind* (2013) document the discourse on the use of neuroscience to assess and direct behaviours; this publication gives public policy a human manipulative role without addressing the breadth of controversy, variability and flux governing moral and behaviour options. The questioning of the capacity of humans to make moral progress by John Gray in *The Silence of Animals* (2013) is well argued and has received considerable publicity. However the book goes no further with the thesis than to recommend a personal response of acceptance and living unquestioningly in the present simply for the sensation of doing so. Options for a societal response are absent and there is no reference to any locus for public policy.

What is lacking in these and other publications is a broader discussion of the role of morality in the light of early 21st-century understanding of human behaviour, and, in particular, discussion of the relationship between morality and public policy. We are not talking here about a moral rationale for a particular policy stance, but rather about how public policy should interconnect with a fluid moral sphere; how it should enhance understanding of the role of morality and respond to its functions and pressure points. This policy book is intended to frame such a debate in the context of British society.

The intention is not to impose the straitjacket of coherence and an all-encompassing solution on the chaotic nature of human behaviours and predispositions, but rather to recognise that humans will construct moral codes that are fluid and frequently at odds, changing over time, place and persons. In the context of social living these codes will require some rationalisation. Morality is about order, but is unstable – a slippery commodity that is contested and mutates. It is likely to remain like that despite scientific explorations of its derivation because its manifestation in any circumstances is contingent on culture and culture's shifts, differences and jostling. It is morality's intrinsic concern with order alongside a propensity to be the subject of friction that points to the benefit of some element of formal, transparent association with public policy.

Morality pervades every part of life and cannot be cut adrift without reference to the way in which life is ordered collectively. The imperative for that connection to be made openly in a reflexive and inclusive manner is the point of principal that will inform the discussion in this book. The need to appraise the relationship has arisen both because of current tensions in the moral sphere and because secularisation has left the UK state bereft of an explicit association with the conceptualisation of morality. One of the consequences of this lack of association has been a tendency for governmental responses to pressures for change to be sluggish and haphazard, with examples ranging from the drive towards equality across social relations, to the quest to liberalise the law relating to abortion and assisted dying, to concerns over rising material inequality. The aim of this study is to analyse this inadequacy of association between morality in its totality, as currently understood and experienced, and public policy – and to instigate a rectification of the shortfalls.

Background

Tensions

The need to reappraise the relationship between morality and public policy in the UK has arisen over time as relations between the two have become increasingly dislocated. Shifts in moral stances have frequently been half understood and resented by a public policy establishment with a residual unsatisfactory umbilical cord to the Christian church; that cord has had a hold on pushes for moral change across the regulation of personal relationships from gay rights to assisted dying. The imperative to facilitate an understanding of moral questions in the public policy sphere has been compounded by significant pressures resulting from the escalation of antagonistic religiosity and secularism alongside scientific advances affecting the core of human identity such as the creation of life and protraction of living. The mainstreaming of human rights within public administration and societal relations has constituted an additional significant dimension. Furthermore, individualism, communication and multicultural living have all mushroomed, while there has been a diminution of societal glue consequent on a whittling away of belief in humanity's capacity to deliver an increasingly caring and fair living environment.

Tensions across human need, expectation, motivation and behaviour are multiple and ageless, but there are time specific points of fracture when the volume of discord notches up sufficiently to suggest the necessity for a better accommodation to be sought. The present is such a time.

Religion and secularism

One of the core tensions to bedevil the 21st century has been the relationship between theistic belief and atheism. To be sure this particular split has been in evidence over centuries and Matthew Arnold's image of declining religion in 'Dover Beach' written in 1867 has been a long-lived refrain.

> The Sea of Faith
> Was once, too, at the full, and round earth's shore
> Lay like the folds of a bright girdle furled.
> But now I only hear
> Its melancholy, long, withdrawing roar,
> Retreating, to the breath
> Of the night-wind, down the vast edges drear
> And naked shingles of the world.

Yet, despite its pedigree, the split between belief and non-belief is currently an issue of such large proportions that it appears to be novel affecting as it does all aspects of social living from medical ethics to education. There has been a surprising widening of the divide and unexpected discord, possibly as a consequence of secular irritation at the capacity of religion to continue its hold on society, and militant atheists have appeared on the scene engendering a vociferous public debate.

The militant atheists have been highly articulate and emotionally engaged in furthering their cause. They have organisations committed to their aims such as the British Humanist Association with numerous eminent supporters. While members of the British Humanist Association are concerned to celebrate human life, their rhetoric is largely oriented around a searing antipathy to religion, its roots in metaphysical beliefs, habitual social conservatism and access to establishment and societal influence.

The atheists can name renowned polemicists such as Christopher Hitchins amongst their number, but perhaps their most celebrated advocate has been the evolutionary biologist Richard Dawkins. In publications such as *The Blind Watchmaker* (Dawkins, 1986) and

The Selfish Gene (Dawkins, 1976) Dawkins propounds and develops Darwinism and a scientific understanding of the human condition – an evolutionary, natural selection and gene-oriented world perspective. Within his argument morality is derived from an empathetic genetic bias supporting human society.

Much of Dawkins' writing is a creative and positive contribution to understanding the human environment. His repudiation of religion has received support from eminent thinkers such as James Watson and Steven Pinker, who endorsed his publication *The God Delusion* (2006), but inevitably there have been critics. The condemnation of religion has been viewed as over negative by Peter Higgs, the scientist and Higgs Bosun theorist (Jha, 2012), and Dawkins' assertion that religion fuels fanaticism and bigotry has incensed a religious establishment and a defensive alliance across faith systems. Counter assertions to bolster the rationale for religion have been made in the context of Christian intellectual thought with publications such as *Dawkins Delusion* (McGrath and McGrath, 2007), and significantly the sales of bibles and religious texts appear to have grown substantially (Smith, 2007). The pot has been stirred and there have been vitriolic exchanges with fundamentalist Christians, in particular creationists. An example has been the widely publicised exchange of Dawkins versus A.E. Wilder-Smith and Edgar Andrews in the Oxford University Huxley memorial debate in 1986.

In terms of chicken and egg – which came first vocal religiosity or militant atheism, the evidence points to a ratchet-up of the former across faiths independently of writers like Dawkins. If an attribution of cause and effect is to be made in a confused interrelationship, it appears to have been the rise of strident religiosity that has set the agenda to a considerable degree prompting a backlash from secularists who had hitherto believed that they were winning through a process of attrition.

Beyond the crumbling of belief witnessed by Matthew Arnold in his poetic lament, the early and mid 20th century saw an overt repudiation of religion in some of the communist and fascist dictatorships, alongside a becalming of religious influence as a predominantly secular state grew in reach and social significance elsewhere. The residual influence of religion was more pronounced in some countries, such as Germany, than others, such as the UK. Perhaps the most surprising implementation of secularism as a self-consciously articulated mode for government was in two countries where religion across a variety of faiths is pervasive – India and Turkey.

India and Turkey with their high levels of religiosity in the context of a formally endorsed secular state mirror to a degree the relationship between religion and the state in the United States. The American constitution specifies the detachment of state and religion, but religion has had a strong hold on the ethos of the country from the Christian commitment of the founding fathers through to the surge in evangelical sects and a range of faiths associated with multiple sources of migration. The interplay between religion and secularism is by this token a complexity of intermeshing trends.

Despite, or perhaps because of, secularism's manifestation in these various governmental formulations, religion has reasserted itself to become a major feature of the 21st-century narrative. An escalation in religious fundamentalism has presented across religions including Buddhism, Christianity, Hinduism, Islam, Judaism, Sikhism and neo-Confucianism (Emerson and Hartman, 2006). What are the perceived causes and traits of the growth in vocal religiosity that has so bestirred the secular lobby to militant atheism and what is its relevance to the tensions affecting the management of morality?

Avakian (2007), in his study *Why is Religious Fundamentalism Growing?*, suggests that a significant contributory cause of 21st-century fundamentalism has been the diminution of other systems of aspiration. The decline in communism as a focus for mass discontent following the collapse of the Soviet Union is the particular case in point. Religious fundamentalism across a range of religions has made an offer of hope, and the urbanisation of the poor has further fuelled the process. The decline of trust in secular progress has undoubtedly been a major influence in the surge in religiosity. Disaffection with communism with no secular replacement to support the disaffected is highly pertinent, but possibly there is also a general perception that secularism as currently realised is mean sustenance for the soul. Certainly there is evidence of resistance to 'modernity' including materialism, the fragmentation of social interaction and the relativity of multiculturalism (Berger, 1992; Bruce 2000; Emerson and Hartman 2006).

John Micklethwait and Adrian Wooldridge (2010) *God is Back. How the Global Rise of Faith is Changing the World*

As with many global shifts in perceptions, attitudes and behaviours, there are multi-layered and varied subtle influences at play. While some may be closely linked, there are also prompts from very different sources. John Micklethwait and Adrian Wooldridge (2010) have conducted an extensive overview of the derivation and impact of a 'global rise' in faith identifying a range of influences operating in the 21st century. They have cited the major role played by the waning of communism in refocusing discontent into the spiritual sphere, alongside the repudiation of modernity by a broad coalition of the socially conservative and those who reject materialism. They have also noted that there has been a turning to religion by those supporting capitalism, but seeking to control the excess of behavioural licence that appears to have emerged as a by product of the operation of the free market; the neo- conservatives in the United States, responding to the perceived lack of restraint amongst the sixties generation, have sought to re-instil bourgeois values of self discipline through promoting the churches and religious faith.

In addition to the communist versus free market divide, Micklethwait and Wooldridge have identified other global influences. They have recognised the potency of an age of democracy when religious commitment amongst population groups has been given the oxygen of advocacy and expression associated with the ballot box. As religion has become increasingly enmeshed in politics in an era of increased democracy from Russia and Eastern Europe to the states of Africa, the Middle East and the Indian sub-continent – so it has gained momentum.

Micklethwait and Wooldridge have also emphasised the role of pluralism in an age when knowledge of a range of religious options is available through global media and connections. As populations are able to own and opt for preferences, their commitment is frequently enhanced. The export of the American model of a vocal commitment to personal religion by the populous – in contrast to a secular European intellectual elite – is factored in. So, too, is the competitive nature of religion bidding for support amongst enfranchised populations.

Migration has been a further highly significant catalyst for the expression of religiosity in secular European countries such as the UK. The influx of citizens from religious Asian and African communities has presented a post Second World War European and certainly British society, wedded to rationalism as its route to redemption after plummeting the depths of bellicosity, with a quandary. How to address different cultural and religious norms have beset administrations with various assimilation and aspirational routes pursued. Racism, prejudice and feelings of ostracism have driven up the expression of religiosity as an action of community solidarity and defiance in the face of a perception of an oppressive host society. Thus, while a first generation of immigrants may embrace a degree of relaxation of expressions of religious conformity, there is evidence of second generations becoming more orthodox than their parents. The process of rebellion has been further fuelled by the negative reaction of a secular intellectual elite that has criticised Islam in particular for aspects of what are perceived as oppressive cultural practices.

And, of course, entwined with all these social movements is realpolitik, nationalism and tribalism with a momentum that increases the profile of religion and taking of sides. Religion has been part and parcel of power struggles across countries ranging from the Indian Pakistan divide and territorial struggle over Kashmir to territorial conflict in Israel, the Sunni Shia conflicts within Islamic communities, insurgent democratic movements linked to religion across the Middle East and the role of American interventions from a conservative white vocally Christian political wing (Micklethwait and Wooldridge, 2010).

> Religious choice has a profound effect on public life. The more that people choose their religion, rather than just inherit it, the more likely they are to make a noise about it. If you have made a commitment to your faith, why would you leave it in the closet at home, or outside the voting booth? At its most basic, that commitment can be violent. Since 2000, 43 per cent of civil wars have been religious. (The figure in the 1940s and 1950s was only about a quarter.) But the main weapon is often the ballot box. Around the world, people have frequently chosen to exercise their new freedoms by increasing, not decreasing, the role of religion in politics. The newly democratised, from Moscow to Cairo to Beijing, have reinserted God back into the public square – and the profoundly secular foreign policy establishment in the West has struggled to deal with it. (Micklethwait and Wooldridge, 2010, p 24)

UK state and public life

Predominantly moderate, but with a connection to the extremes of fundamentalism, the tensions between religion and secularism have been played out across the UK's structures of state and public life. There are high profile disputes over the degree to which the UK is a Christian country such as that triggered by the Prime Minister David Cameron's pledge of state support for an established Christian church (Cameron, 2014). A perhaps surprisingly vociferous response in the *Telegraph* newspaper from secularists with leading positions in society across social administration, business, academia and the arts gives an indication of the raw edge of the religious atheistic debate:

> Apart from in the narrow constitutional sense that we continue to have an established church, Britain is not a 'Christian Country'. Repeated surveys, polls and studies show that most of us as individuals are not Christian in our beliefs or our religious identities. At a social level, Britain has been shaped for the better by many pre-Christian,

non-Christian and post-Christian forces. We are a plural society with citizens with a range of perspectives, and we are largely a non-religious society.

Constantly to claim otherwise fosters alienation and division in our society... (*Telegraph*, 2014)

That problematic interface is fuelled, not only by an established faith, but also by multiple faiths demanding recognition in a multicultural society. As a consequence of campaigns, pressures for fair play and a desire to promote spirituality across the spectrum of faith by believers keen to stem the tide of disbelief, there has been a growth in the position of a range of religious groups within the public domain. Broadcasting has slots for multiple faiths; community funding is directed towards religious initiatives; and public administration takes on board faith perspectives in consultations and service provision. But perhaps the area of public life where religiosity has been encouraged and allowed most social influence has been in education. There has been active encouragement of religious schools across faiths by successive governments and they have proliferated. As local authority management of education has been curtailed and the provision of education fragmented, a vacuum has been filled by religious institutions. Fears that this process may have gone too far have been voiced within the education establishment and beyond. These pressures from a range of faiths have led after a period of rapid change to the establishment by the Woolf Institute of the Commission on Religion and Belief in British Public Life (Owen, 2015).

The role accorded to faith in public life has been a running sore for secularists for some time. One of the principal avenues of campaigning by the British Humanist Association (2012; 2014a) has been to voice concern over an increasing public platform and consequent influence for religion with an invisibility of non-faith perspectives. Theirs has been a search for a curtailment of a perceived religious monopoly across communications and policy influence – within parliament, broadcasts, public consultations, schools and more – and an assertion of the voice of secularism (see for example 'Holy redundant. Remove bishops from parliament', *BHA News*, issue 3/2012 and the BHA website, https://humanism.org.uk).

The tensions flagged up here do not simply relate to matters spiritual, the dichotomy of belief and non-belief, potent as these may be in firing up emotions and debate. Significantly they also relate to morality and social intercourse. There is an in-principle divergence in moralities between codes that are derived from revelation, typically associated with metaphysical systems, and those shaped by a human centred model serving perceived human need.

There is an overlap between the two as traditions and cultures are sustained and seep influence over centuries, and the human predicament inevitably pervades both approaches. But a split there nevertheless is which has implications for tensions in the moral sphere and ipso facto the state's role in managing these. A sustained and fundamental fracture between these two thematic strands of morality relates to the degree of flexibility with which they respond to changes in social mores. Humanistic, secular moralities are likely to adapt moral precepts more rapidly to accommodate changes in social attitudes, behaviours and impinging circumstances because their raison d'être is to facilitate living. Revelatory systems have a purpose beyond humanity – to fulfil the objects of a being or reality beyond the material world; once revealed precepts supporting such a purpose are hard to modify.

There are incidents of this tension between social flexibility and social conservatism associated with the secular religious divide that have had a major impact on the governance of morality in the UK particularly in respect of personal relations. The saga is of ongoing resistance in the face of the push for changes in legislation. Examples include the facilitation of divorce, the legalisation of abortion, equalities legislation across gender and sexual orientation differences and the permitting of certain scientific advances to support the extension of life and the relief of pain and suffering. It has been a resistance frequently, though not exclusively, in the face of majority popular support for change. Possibly the most striking example of where resistance from a socially conservative religious establishment has successfully stalled the implementation of a change desired by most of the population has been in respect of assisted dying. The points of contention are multiple and complex, with reservations expressed, for example, by the disability lobby and some branches of the medical profession. Nevertheless the objection voiced by faith groups has been a significant obstacle over the years (Church of England, 2014). An example of multi-faith opposition can be seen in the *Assisted dying: Faith leaders' statement* (Faith Leaders, 2014) involving 24 signatories across faith groups in the UK – Christian, Jewish, Muslim, Sikh, Buddhist, Jain and Zoroastrian faiths.

Cultural flux and individualism

There are characteristics of post-modern society that exacerbate this antithesis between secularism and religion resulting in raw friction with gladiatorial overtones in the public arena. Increased communication and knowledge of different cultural behaviours has the potential to augment negative as well as positive responses to difference. Population movements that bring different moral perspectives into close proximity have similar potential outcomes. Sexual mores, attitudes towards gender equality, sexual orientation, elder care and familial duty all feature as points of difference between cultural groups sufficient to draw extensive publicity.

There is, too, the reach of individualism in a post-modern society which sets store on individual fulfilment and self-determination. The ability to see what others do and aspire to, with all the variety that is on offer, is enhanced in an era of mass communication. Individualism is catching. It is potentially disruptive across cultures with traditionalism assailed in the face of generational and idiosyncratic challenges. Intergenerational change is not new, but mass communication has increased the speed with which it happens. The sixties are often described as the era when the rate of change moved up a gear, and shifts in sexual and intergenerational behaviour and perceptions of acceptability as mapped by the British Social Attitudes survey have continued in the latter part of the 20th and into the 21st centuries (Duncan and Phillips, 2008; Hunt, 2009; NatCen, 2014).

Individual materialism versus communal obligation

There are also tensions in two spheres of social functioning, which, while they may be recognised as a permanent feature of human society, have become particularly acute in the 21st century. The first relates to the conflicting impulses towards individual material acquisition on the one hand and communal obligation, sharing and fostering equality on the other. The emergent consensus during and after the Second World War was towards a greater emphasis on social good and equality; for example the establishment of the National Health Service and other features of the welfare state had cross party support (Beveridge, 1942). Greater equality in the distribution of wealth was achieved through a combination of full employment, growth in gross domestic product and a redistributive taxation and benefits system (Jago, 2014). However, as the welfare consensus diminished in the wake of the advent of economic neo-liberalism, a wealthy global class and a range of income disparities, society was confronted with a new reality of growing and out of control inequality. In some quarters there is acquiescence in this new phenomena, in others it is abhorred. More generally there is a heightened level of anxiety that the received socioeconomic model in which the world now deals is unmanageable in terms of delivering on the human impulse of bolstering social equality and caring (Piketty, 2014).

Human conduct

This tension is matched by a second rather less theorised but nevertheless pervasive disquiet concerning the continued mismatch between the expectations and reality of human conduct. Following the social collapse and unleashing of destruction and sadism in the Second World War there was in the motivation of rebuilding the imperative of sustaining a conviction that change was achievable. The belief that moral 'progress' in society could be achieved through the panoply of education, welfare, physical and mental health props, and organisational and social policing and exhortation was a sustaining narrative. That narrative has worn thin in the face, not only of subsequent war conflicts and associated atrocities, but also in the repeated incidents of corruption, theft in multiple guises, cover-ups, intrusions into privacy, smears and bullying across public and private institutions where expectation of services are at a very low ebb (NatCen, 2013). Possibly most damaging to the conviction of moral progress in a society committed in rhetoric to the wellbeing of its citizens has been the abuse and cruelty in evidence in caring institutions. Adjustment to the realisation that the 'bad egg' explanation will not do is particularly hard in respect of crimes viewed as out of the ordinary evil that have extracted the maximum howl of disgust. Paedophilia falls within this category as its pervasiveness becomes increasingly apparent.

Challenge

Such an assortment of differences and tensions in the moral sphere as have been described here present a colossal challenge if a society is to cohere – and certainly not one to be pushed under the carpet. Responding effectively is increasingly an imperative for government and yet it is an imperative that is largely unrecognised and is certainly met with a response that falls short of legitimate expectation.

Government deficit

These tensions concerning change and oppositional cultures have thrown into sharp relief the inadequacy of the governance of morality in the UK. Deemed a prickly customer, morality is habitually relegated to the best-avoided backroom of government operations. While railings against moral failings feature in the media and on political platforms, there is little formal, measured consideration of the broad state of moral play; certainly there is no facility for taking an overview of developments with an expectation of a timely and effective administrative response. As a result the moral dimension to perplexing social issues such as resource distribution and institutional functioning receives inadequate attention, and there is a gap in understanding that is particularly detrimental to a society's potential to negotiate the moral changes affecting personal relations and existential questions of life, death and human identity.

The example of assisted dying

There are many instances where this deficiency has had a negative impact that might be cited by way of illustration, but the fraught issue of assisted dying presents a particularly stark and highly topical example and is consequently considered here in some detail. It offers a saga of the failure of government to attend to one of the most high profile, burning issues of the day — whether medical assistance should be available to assist the self-administration of lethal drugs in the event of a patient's settled wish to die in the face of a terminal illness. We have witnessed a split between public opinion supporting a change in the law, on the one hand, and strong faith and other lobbyist support for the status quo on the other, and, in the absence of an executive lead, recourse by advocates of change to vulnerable private members bills and a series of attempts to modify the impact of existing law through judicial applications and test cases.

Public attitudes surveys have shown growing support for assisted dying with a ComRes survey in 2010 finding that 73 per cent considered that family and friends should not be prosecuted for helping a loved one to die and 74 per cent that a medical professional should be legally permitted to help patients end their lives. Yet despite public attitudes, which should themselves have triggered a government review of the appropriateness of the law as it stands, there has been an absence of a major, in principle government initiative. Filling the vacuum have been failed attempts by Patricia Hewitt and Lord Falconer to introduce an amendment to the Coroners and Justice Bill 2008/9, Lord Joffe's private members bill in 2006, which fell before being examined in detail, and the private members bill introduced by Lord Falconer currently before the house, which, despite interest exhibited in the House of Lords, runs the risk of not reaching House of Commons debate because of a lack of government backing.

Through the latter half of the 20th century a process of avoidance by the executive had delivered an uncertain legal situation where assisting someone to take their own life was illegal under the Suicide Act 1961, but the prosecution of relatives when they had provided such assistance had been, in the event, unlikely. This prompted recourse to judicial interpretation with a number of high profile cases seeking a ruling in favour of an individual being able to receive help to die. Acting on a House of Lords ruling in the Debbie Purdy case, which indicated concern that the European Convention on Human Rights (ECHR) tests of 'accessibility and foreseeability' were not being met in the absence of a clear policy, the Department for Public Prosecutions published a policy statement in February 2010. While this confirmed that the prosecution of relatives acting in good faith in respect of someone who was terminally ill would be unlikely, the humanitarian benefit of having a doctor involved in providing assistance through medication was not catered for (Lipscombe and Barber, 2014).

Tony Nicklinson who had locked-in syndrome took a case to the Supreme Court arguing that the prohibition of medical assistance with dying contravened his human right to a private and family life. While Nicklinson's claim was not upheld, the court stressed the importance of parliamentary review of an unsatisfactory situation rather than a continued ducking of the issue. Furthermore, the possibility of a successful human rights claim in the future was noted.

While there has been a Commission on Assisted Dying, it has been undertaken wholly outside government auspices hosted by the think tank Demos and sponsored by assisted dying supporters Terry Pratchett and Bernard Lewis. What was needed was an in depth, detailed government sponsored review examining public attitudes and shifting moral perspectives, the scientific reality of prolonged life, the operation of the current law and evidence from precedents of legalised assisted dying in other jurisdictions. Instead, this complex and emotive subject has been left to resolution through the undignified spectacle of a public tug of war between protagonists on both sides seeking to frighten and emote in favour of their proposition. In favour of the status quo we have had the powerful faith establishment, the disability lobby and a branch of the medical profession – the Royal College of Surgeons. In the other corner, those presenting the case for change have included people who have been prevented from dying and who have campaigned from a position of acute distress together with their supporters operating through lobby groups such as Dignity in Dying. In the absence of a substantive government review there has been a public relations exercise displayed on both sides. The failure of government to establish a review over such a long period of time has engendered mistrust so that were one to be set in motion at this late stage it might be viewed as a delaying tactic. Indeed such a motive might be attributed to the Church of England, which has had to change tack and call for an inquiry in the face of two senior clerics altering their opinions to now favour assisted dying – the former Archbishop George Carey and Bishop Desmond Tutu (BBC, 2014a).

The consequences of this dereliction of government duty span debilitating uncertainty within the judicial system, heightened anxiety within the medical profession and the unedifying spectacle of the terminally ill having to travel abroad to end their lives; 292 have made the journey to the Dignitas euthanasia clinic in Switzerland since 2002 (Doward, 2015), while governments have for two decades avoided undertaking the substantive review that the issue merits.

Further examples – abortion, homosexuality, resource distribution and social management

The distressing tale of assisted dying is by no means unique. It is repeated across governmental handling of questions of life and death, personal relations and even the core stuff of politics – resource distribution and social management. A few examples are flagged up here prior to further probing in Chapter Four.

- The harmful delay in addressing assisted dying was mirrored in the early post war decades in respect of abortion. The price in human suffering of an inappropriate law criminalising any termination of pregnancy has been well documented and indeed portrayed in films such as Mike Leigh's 2004 production of *Vera*, the tragedy of a 1950s back street abortionist. The consequence of a dilatory government response was a toll of botched abortions. The faith establishment opposed change and the government side-stepped the issue with change yet again being dependent on being introduced via a private member's bill.
- The regulation of personal relationships has been similarly subject to a procrastinated response. Extraordinarily homosexuality remained subject to legal sanctions until 1967. Subsequently, despite the legalisation of homosexual relations, it took until 2005 for civil partnerships to be introduced, and it is noteworthy that regulatory support for heterosexual cohabitees has still not been established denying vulnerable partners adequate financial protection (Fairbairn, 2014).

- A further moral sphere where minimal government engagement with morality has had a detrimental impact relates to issues associated with wealth distribution and lack of what might be termed moral progress in the operation of institutions and behaviour. Post war expectations of a more equal and protective society have faltered. They have done so against a backdrop of limited shared understanding of the moral questions involved. The absence of such an understanding informing public debate has had the impact of disempowering collective decision-making. We are not necessarily talking here about shifts in morality over time with which governments have failed to keep pace, but rather a failure to review core issues in the context of a broader conceptual understanding of morality and the management of contradictory impulses. Facilitating such an understanding would have some possibility of diminishing the degree to which society feels in shock and flounders unable to respond in the face of inadequately explained outcomes and behaviours; the notion of progress itself needs re-assessment from the position of a deeper appreciation of how human beings and their moralities actually operate.

Historical roots of governance deficiency

An historical perspective is needed to understand why there is such an unsatisfactory interface between the state and morality, and a failure of government to properly discharge its responsibilities in the moral sphere. The reluctance to engage can in part be traced back to the relationship between the Christian church and the UK state, which has dwindled over time leading to the current unsatisfactory residual umbilical cord. The Christian church's relationship with the state in the UK, as elsewhere, has been long. In its early stages it was intense, albeit that the institutions were at times at loggerheads, embittered and estranged. Latterly it has become distant with a residual nostalgia and deference towards an historical bond largely sustained for symbolic purposes; nevertheless there are elements of residual power.

Intensity certainly belonged to the Middle Ages with conversion to the faith steered through kingly example, where we even have accession to kingly sainthood in Edward the Confessor. To be sure, there was a separate power base in the church, but the dedication to a Christian point of reference was total and unquestioned amongst the laity despite episodic turbulence such as the Becket Henry II impasse and the protestant property grab and iconoclasm of the Tudor and civil war eras. While there was case specific defiance of moral codes, such as the marital shenanigans of Henry VIII, the public point of reference was a Christian one across the operation of state affairs.

The strains in dual power based governance gave way over time and after various stressful junctures to equilibrium with the state being the locus of power within a Christian dominion. There was no disestablishment of the church; there was no declared establishment of a secular state. Rather there was a withering on the vine of a belief-oriented public estate so that in the 20th and 21st centuries the state no longer did religion to any meaningful degree.

Nevertheless the trappings remained. Most notable of these is the Christian church presence in the House of Lords with a voluble political voice and expectation of deference on points of moral behaviour. Some 26 prelates sit on the cross benches. To this gradualist legacy may be attributed the tendency of the state to side step questions of moral principle leaving statements of this nature to the church. The contention in this discussion is that such reliance on a diminishing religious edifice is no longer a tenable situation. With the range of tensions about the nature and direction of morality confronting 21st century society, a process of comprehensive governmental review is required.

Some instances can be cited where government has bowed to pressures and has begun to engage in some, albeit limited, institutional assessment of morality. There are, for example, international human rights that cannot be separated from government having been created for the control of state oppression after the Second World War. To be sure the primary subject of rights being concerned with entitlements is only tangentially related to morality. But entitlements imply delivery obligations and duties − the stuff of morality. Human rights and the structures that have been created to secure adherence to the tenets of the European Convention on Human Rights, such as the Human Rights Act (1998) and the Equality and Human Rights Commission, have become a point of reference for public administration, which, in turn, has had some impact on the degree to which morality is necessarily the subject of governmental consideration.

There is also a challenge coming from the imposition of change on the life project through scientific invention constituting a further lever edging government towards intervention. The ability to prolong life and to manipulate, shape and even create humans through genetic and other interventions requires regulation in unchartered moral territory. There has been some recognition of the need for a reflexive public policy resource in respect of the moral precepts that apply to scientific developments with the establishment of the Emerging Science and

Bioethics Committee. There are also examples of short-term inquiries considering the frontiers of specific ethical issues such as the Committee of Inquiry into Human Fertilisation and Embryology chaired by the philosopher Mary Warnock. However, by their nature these institutions have an issue specific, limited remit within the sphere of morality.

The 21st-century moral pressure pot

In sum the tensions and diversity in moral theory and practice have been heightened in the 21st century by the faith secular divide, multicultural living, individualism, intergenerational shifts, the catalyst of burgeoning communication facilities and issues of resource distribution and behaviour management. Together they constitute a state of change and fracture that demands a considered, comprehensive governmental response, but to date this has not been forthcoming, albeit that there has been some activity prompted by administrative pressures – for example in respect of human rights and the impact of science on the human life course and identity.

Aim

The object of the discussion in this book is to contribute to rectifying this governmental deficit in the UK. The endeavour is to produce a model for the state's role in supporting and managing morality with its attendant fluidity, multiple codes and frictions in a fast changing, multicultural society. Reflecting on the causes of morality, its shifts, tensions, differences and common features, the argument is based on the premise that morality is not simply concerned with the promotion of empathetic responses, but is rather engaged with the accommodation of a wide range of long- and short-term human impulses, some of which are convergent and some divergent, within varied and changing cultural contexts. The contention is that these would benefit from synchronisation in the public policy arena. While the proposals are intended to address the tensions in morality, it is not anticipated that they will be resolved if by being resolved the aspiration is to iron them out. For example, it is not suggested that there be recourse to a utilitarian approach in order to weigh up differences as proposed by Greene (2014) in his book *Moral Tribes: Emotion, Reason and the Gap between Us and Them*. Motivations, influences and cultural traditions are too complex for that. Rather the intention is to live with difference with some modus vivendi being sought.

The model proposed is grounded in a recognition of the need to incorporate in public policy discourse as full an understanding of morality as is feasible including a wide variety of perceptions. Stimulating reflexive debate and according the conceptualisation of morality a higher profile within public policy is a significant component of the approach. Although the intention is to facilitate acknowledgement of uncomfortable challenges to certainties and conventions, the value and inevitability of cultural and behavioural continuities is recognised. There is scepticism of the ultimate solution aspirations of some moral systems and life interpretations, but the stance adopted is not to discard frameworks that assist living, but to recognise them for what they are – their scope and contribution.

In summary the aim is to define the role of public policy in relation to reviewing morality and responding to its functions and pressure points. A core purpose of the exercise is to enhance the capacity of governments to manage morality and to respond flexibly and in a more timely fashion to shifts in social mores and moral perceptions within different cultural circumstances.

Content

The book comprises six chapters leading through an assessment of the nature of morality and its relationship with government to consideration of options to enhance public policy responses. It is focused on the UK, but inevitably draws on aspects of a wider global context.

Following the introduction, the second chapter, 'Moral perspectives to be addressed in an inclusive public policy', comprises an analysis of core moral themes that are pertinent to the discussion including:

- *revelatory* systems which encompass religious and theistic beliefs through to convictions associated with a de-personalised life force;
- systems of *moral philosophy* concerned principally with fulfilment either as an individual or collectively as a society involving a process of rationalisation;
- the developing field of *scientific analysis* involving naturalistic observations, psychological analyses of human impulses and neurological investigations into the operation of the brain and behaviours;
- strands of thinking concerned with *commonality* across moral systems; and

- *relativism*. Somewhat in contrast to advocates of commonality in morality have been exponents of divergence often associated with liberalism and the endorsement of a tolerant, individualistic society.

The third chapter considers the interconnection of these strands of thought – the synergy and tensions, and the need for some element of accommodation in relation to the public policy interface. The contention is made that morality is not a simple promoter of the social instincts, but rather a manager of the human condition. The emerging proposition that morality is concerned with the accommodation of impulses within varied and changing cultural contexts combines a degree of commonality and relativism that, it is argued, would benefit from recognition and synchronisation in the public policy arena.

Chapter Four, 'The challenges and benefits of a new role for public policy', explores the implications of this approach. The proposal to establish formal consideration and debate of morality as a public policy function in conjunction with a recognition that morality is about the accommodation of a wide spectrum of impulses rather than offering a trajectory of progress is examined in terms of the challenges and benefits to public policy.

The penultimate chapter, 'Managing morality – a public policy analytical tool', considers the proposition that inter-cultural and generational moral tensions would have an enhanced opportunity for accommodation with the establishment of an official body for the purpose of ongoing review of the public policy morality interface. A range of options concerning the remit, status and modus operandi of such a body are put forward for consideration. This is then followed by a final concluding chapter that draws the argument and proposals together with pointers for the direction of future debate.

TWO

Moral perspectives to be addressed in an inclusive public policy

The kaleidoscope of morality is daunting for the analyst trying to get a handle on the myriad of thoughts, emotions, habits and cultural identities that fall within its domain. A full description is beyond the scope or indeed the purpose of this discussion. Rather the task is to draw out the core themes of division and coherence in morality that critically need to be assessed in order to develop a positive interface with public policy.

In this chapter synergies and oppositional pulls are drawn out to facilitate this objective. We examine two broad thematic splits that require acknowledgement and accommodation. The *first* of these is between revelatory systems of thought espousing the metaphysical, on the one hand, and, on the other, a humanistic orientation with rationalist philosophical thinking on the subject of morals, fulfilment and happiness. The *second* relates to a narrative of commonality in understanding and bettering the operation of morality versus a relativistic stance that abjures the common thread and instead opts for an interpretation of morality that is culturally and individually determined. Finally scientific insights across these dimensions are considered forming a fifth component of this review of different models of moral development and understanding.

Revelatory morality

The arguments marshalled in the field of revelatory morality relate to the metaphysical rather than rational deduction or human psychology. That is not to say that they are irrational or that they are wholly divorced of human imaging and needs, but rather that the final arbiter lies outside the material world and human control and even understanding.

Revelatory morality has largely been within the purview of religion; it is described in the Oxford Dictionary as 'the belief in and worship of a superhuman controlling power, especially a personal God or gods'. There have been in the past and continue to be a multiplicity of religions manifesting a diverse cultural heritage. In terms of global population numbers adhering to their tenets, the principal religions that have continued to hold sway in the 21st century are Buddhism (7.1 per cent), Christianity (31.5 per cent), Hinduism (15.0 per cent) and Islam (23.2 per cent). Believers in folk religions encompass 5.9 per cent and 0.8 per cent adhere to other religions (Pew Research Center, 2012). Monotheism is the predominant form of religion, but all institutional religion is typified by some form of personification of what is perceived as a metaphysical truth, whether a god in human form or a human conduit for a divine message. While most people acknowledge a religious affiliation, a substantial proportion of the global population is unaffiliated to any institutional religion, some 16.3 per cent. They comprise, as well as atheists and agnostics, those who have a belief in an undefined spiritual force (Pew Research Center, 2012).

While levels of religious affiliation are hard to calculate and cited statistics need to be treated with caution particularly when emanating from religious foundations, there is evidence from polls of an increase in the percentage of the global population with religious affiliations (Micklethwaite and Wooldridge, 2010). One study from the World Christian Database which Micklethwaite and Woodridge cite found that affiliation to the four largest world religions – Buddhism, Christianity, Hinduism and Islam – increased from 67 per cent in 1900 to 73 per cent in 2005 with further rises anticipated over the coming decades. While some of this may be explained by moves from smaller tribal religions to larger religions, the findings are nevertheless significant. Overall there does not appear to be a growth in individuals with secular convictions outside Europe.

In addition to the considerable scale of religious adherence across the globe, the 20th and 21st centuries have seen a growth in fundamentalist and vocal religiosity. In America, for example, the tolerant Episcopal Church has declined in favour of evangelical Southern Baptists. A highly charged Christian fundamentalism, Pentecostalism, founded in America, has thrived globally frequently at the expense of mainstream Catholicism. Currently this movement (Pentecostalism) is estimated to have 500 million participants (Pew Research Center, 2006). Hindu and Islamic fundamentalism has also thrived with, for example, the Hindu political movement in India and the well-documented social conservatism of Islamic states such as Iran and Saudi Arabia. This religiosity has manifested itself in adversarialism that has included cultural stand offs and on occasion warfare. It is in evidence in respect of, for example, Catholicism versus Protestant evangelicalism, Sunni versus Shia formulations of Islam, and defensive stances between the major religions – Christianity, Islam, Hinduism, Judaism, Sikhism and Buddhism (Micklethwaite and Wooldridge, 2010).

In the UK the number declaring a religious affiliation is far lower than the global figure, with 50.6 per cent claiming to have no religion in the most recent British Social Attitudes Survey (NatCen, 2014). Some 42 per cent acknowledged a Christian belief, but affiliation to the established church, the Church of England, has declined from some 36 per cent in 1985 to about 20 per cent in 2012 (NatCen, 2014). While religious belief is declining in this country, religion nevertheless remains at the forefront of national debate on moral issues.

Multifaceted, contradictory – religion reflects life and human impulses

For many people religion provides the most vivid and fulfilling host for morality. It offers an aid to living through narrative, myth, art, music and theatre, and it assuages fear by offering the prospect of an afterlife. It addresses the breadth and tensions in the human psyche and frequently does so with *dramatis personae*.

There are the wars of the gods and the acting out of multiple passions in Greek and Norse myths. There is original sin, the fall of mankind, the dichotomy between good and evil personified in the fight between god and the devil in the Christian religious construction. The Manichean religion offers a scenario where the empires of good and evil as powers in the universe clash with the world as the battlefield. Matter – earth – is evil and base, and withdrawal from earthly matters and engagement with the spirit through a variety of devices such as fasting and contemplation is espoused, as in many religions (Midgley, 1984). This particular aspect of religious vision is one of winning the fight; good should vanquish evil, and evil is a force in the world to be reckoned with. It is a conception that has guilt, chastisement and corporeal loathing as its baggage. There is something here of human passions and a sense of the apocalyptic associated with muddled, out of control psychological drivers and mortality.

It is significant that in responding to human impulses a number of religions, predominantly pantheistic and polytheistic, do not have a good/evil split, and even where such a split does exist, predominantly within monotheism, there are a host of contexts and contradictory impulses worthy of note (Assmann, 2004). The wealth of the impulses that religion caters for goes beyond the 'fight' to other inclinations. For example, there is torture, which has a thematic hold on Christian practice from the centrality of the crucifixion to the martyrdom of the saints. Then there are the elaborate rituals of pain – hell on earth and hell in the afterlife. There is much engagement in the spectacle of pain and sadism – a predilection of the human psyche woven into the fabric of many religions and their moralities. Then there is a thread through morality and spiritual practice across cultures of the abnegation of the self – the ascetic life that provides a release from the irksome demands of choice and want. There is, too, in contrast to self-abnegation, self-promotion. In the personalised religions we see the urge to individual distinction, recognition and praise being accommodated. A further example of engagement with conflicting impulses can be seen in the continual tug of war between power, obedience and self-realisation. How central to religious morality is both the bolstering of authority and its challenge – an encapsulation of the emotional drivers and conflict in personal and social relationships. One only needs to look historically at the attitude to inequality in the Christian church – exhortation to the disadvantaged to accept their lot alongside material support for the poor and admonition of the elevated and the wealthy.

Addressing as they do the full gamut of human impulses, it is not surprising that many religious systems are typified by detailed specification of requisite behaviour across matters such as mode of worship, ritual, gender roles, sexual conduct, intergenerational relations, property regulation, blasphemy, doctrinal texts and more.

Furthermore, as noted in Chapter One, the nature of religious morality being grounded in the requirements of a god renders it less malleable and adaptable to change and conciliation than secular moralities. The combination of this trait with detailed behavioural prescription presents a major point of difficulty for the management of morality by a state administration that is seeking to be responsive to social difference and pressures for change.

Growing adherence to a 'life force'

Detailed prescription and inflexibility is less in evidence in respect of looser revelatory moralities associated with a 'life force' rather than personified theism. The notion of some relatively undefined metaphysical being has a long history and appears to be a conviction shared by a substantial proportion of the world's population in the 21st century according to Pew's 2012 survey of religious affiliation. A Eurobarometer poll in 2005 found that in the UK some 40 per cent agreed with the statement that 'there is some sort of life force' (Eurobarometer, 2005).

Looking at Ancient Greece, Plato's ideal forms – the spiritual essence of the material world and ideal to which the latter aspires but falls short of – offers an early, sophisticated conception of a generalised life force

(Ruggiero, 2002). Current advocates concerned with an exploration of the derivation and properties of morality include thinkers such as Ronald Dworkin and Clive Hamilton. The former, coming from a legal human rights background, has written *Religion without God* in which he attributes human values and appreciation of what is right to a metaphysical force. While human perception of that entity is only shadowy, it is sufficiently revealing to sustain moral conviction (Dworkin, 2013). He builds on Einstein's identification of a non-personal god linked to the mysteries of beauty and wisdom, and cites Rudolf Otto's (1958) description of the numinous experience as 'a kind of faith knowledge'.

Hamilton (2008) in his study of 'post secular' ethics draws on the neuroscience finding of an empathetic dimension to the brain to underwrite his conviction of an underlying spiritual force. His interpretation of the nature of morality is that it is broadly affirmative with moral themes holding good across cultures, and that this, in turn, is linked to the wiring of the brain and an intuition that derives from some essence of matter or being beyond the individual and of which all matter is a part – the 'noumenon'.

'Religious atheists' and the 'noumenon'

Ronald Dworkin

What Dawkins misses is that for pantheists a numinous experience is an experience of something they take to be *real*. It is not just an emotional experience whose origin and content may be explained by evolutionary advantage or by some deep psychological need. Pantheists believe there is wonder or beauty or moral truth or meaning or something else of value *in* what they experience. Their reaction is produced by a conviction of value and a response to that conviction; it cannot be accurately understood without recognising that a real value is its object. We should not say that though pantheists – I include Spinoza – do not believe in a personal god, they believe in a non-personal god. It would be much clearer and more accurate to call them religious atheists. (Dworkin, 2013, p 43)

Clive Hamilton

If we can find a fixed point, it will allow a moral philosophy to be nailed down, and moral relativism vanishes. I argue that there is such a locus, a metaphysical absolute that is the basis for all-important moral judgements. After consideration of the alternatives, I adopted the term 'noumenon' (usually pronounced 'noomenon') to describe its source. Kant uses this word for his concept of 'the thing-in-itself', which can be thought of as the world as it is, in its pure existence, before we bring our forms of understanding to it. The noumenon is always discussed as a partner of the concept of the 'phenomenon', the world of everyday appearances. As this suggests, the distinction is really about how we experience and understand the world.

Although fundamental to the work of Kant and Schopenhauer, the distinction between noumenon and phenomenon is more a characteristic of Eastern philosophies, in which the idea of the noumenon is captured in terms such as 'universal essence' and 'subtle essence'. Throughout the book I note some parallels between my argument and those from Eastern traditions, where it has long been understood that the noumenon can be known (if at all) only by transcending the everyday forms of understanding.

Although the noumenon is usually thought of as a characteristic of the world 'out there', I take up Schopenhauer's most original insight (which he subsequently recognised in the classics of Hinduism) that the noumenon must also be found within us. In developing my moral philosophy, I call this fixed point within us 'the moral self' (Hamilton, 2008, p xiii).

Systems of moral philosophy with a genesis in rational argument

There are various systems of moral philosophy that are derived from human cogitation rather than metaphysical revelation. They are generated within the parameters of human philosophical thought with human-oriented objectives. These are systems of moral philosophy concerned principally with human fulfilment either as an individual or collectively as a society involving a process of rationalisation.

Individual fulfilment

In terms of the individual perspective there is a major strand of thought concerned with the search for a good and meaningful life. Aristotle is widely viewed as one of the principal exponents of this philosophical stance and offers a further example of the Ancient Greek origins of European philosophical thought. Aristotle (2004) made the case for the realisation of an individual's capacities, a life engaged with the honing of capabilities and the virtues. Through this route fulfilment could be achieved. It is an approach that has permeated western thinking and today can be seen in the socioeconomic theories of the likes of Amartya Sen (1992). In the same vein, self determined goals with a life plan were advocated by Rawls (1971). Addressing the issue from the perspective of the vagaries of human life, Bernard Williams (1981) considered the realisation of human individual fulfilment in the context of the individual making choices with multiple pressures and influences.

Duty

The notion of duty constitutes a strand of moral philosophy concerned with individual responsibility within the collective. It is an exemplar of post enlightenment ethics based on reason, a negotiated set of expectations developed by philosophers unguided by emotion. Kant (1785) argued that duty formed the crux of morality with a universal set of rules that allowed for no differentiation between cultures or individuals; they were the product of theoretical rationalisation. They were about principles and regulation and did not exist with reference to outcomes or empirical consideration of behaviour, which Schopenhauer (1837), for example, considered a defect.

> An action done from duty has its moral worth, *not in the purpose* to be attained by it, but in the maxim according with which it is decided upon; it depends therefore, not on the realisation of the object of the action, but solely on the *principle of volition* in accordance with which, irrespective of all objects of the faculty of desire, the action has been performed. That the purposes we may have in our actions, and also their effects considered as ends and motives of the will, can give to actions no unconditioned and moral worth is clear from what has gone before. Where then can this worth be found if we are not to find it in the will's relation to the effect hoped for from the action? It can be found nowhere but in the *principle of the will*, irrespective of the ends which can be brought about by such an action; for between its *a priori*, which is formal, and it's *a posteriori* motive, which is material, the will stands, so to speak at a parting of the ways; and since it must be determined by some principle, it will have to be determined by the formal principle or volition when an action is done from duty, when, as we have seen, every material principle is

taken away from it. (Kant, 1785/2005, pp 71–2, emphasis in original)

The case made here for adherence to a code because of duty, irrespective of desire or anticipated outcome, stands in contrast to Russell's perception of the need for unity between reason and the emotions.

> Undoubtedly we should desire the happiness of those whom we love, but not as an alternative to our own. In fact the whole antithesis between self and the rest of the world, which is implied in the doctrine of self-denial, disappears as soon as we have any genuine interest in persons or things outside of ourselves. …
>
> All unhappiness depends upon some kind disintegration or lack of integration; there is disintegration within the self through lack of coordination between the conscious and unconscious mind; there is lack of integration between the self and society where the two are not knit together by the force of objective interests and affections. The happy man is the man who does not suffer from either of these failures of unity, whose personality is neither divided against itself nor pitted against the world. (Russell, 1930/2006, p 175)

While Kant's inflexibility, even sterility, has been critiqued, his concepts have had an influence through to the present day, albeit that they have been considerably modified. Rawls neo-Kantian *Theory of Justice* (1971), for example, proposed the collective development of social rules without those engaged in their development knowing how they would personally be affected – operating from behind what Rawls described as a 'veil of ignorance'.

> The idea of the original position is to set up a fair procedure so that any principles agreed to will be just. The aim is to use the notion of pure procedural justice as a basis of theory. Somehow we must nullify the effects of special contingencies which put men at odds and tempt them to exploit social and natural circumstances to their own advantage. Now in order to do this I assume that the parties are situated behind a veil of ignorance. They do not know how the various alternatives will affect their own particular case and they are obliged to evaluate principles solely on the basis of general considerations. (Rawls, 1971, pp 136–137)

Now the reasons for the veil of ignorance go beyond mere simplicity. We want to define the original position so that we get the desired solution. If a knowledge of particulars is allowed, then the outcome is biased by arbitrary contingencies. As already observed, to each according to his threat advantage is not a principle of justice. If the original position is to yield agreements that are just, the parties must be fairly situated and treated equally as moral persons. The arbitrariness of the world must be corrected for by adjusting the circumstances of the initial contractual situation. Moreover, if in choosing principles we required unanimity even when there is full information, only a few rather obvious cases could be decided. A conception of justice based on unanimity in these circumstances would indeed be weak and trivial. But once knowledge is excluded, the requirement of unanimity is not out of place and the fact that it can be satisfied is of great importance. It enables us to say of the preferred conception of justice that it represents a genuine reconciliation of interests. (Rawls, 1971, p 141–2)

Utilitarianism

One of the principal strands of thought concerned with the collective from an empirical and outcomes perspective is Bentham's societal 'utilitarian' approach, which has the guiding purpose of promoting happiness for the greatest number (Bentham, 1780). The proposition is that social regulation, behaviours and decisions should be adopted that will deliver this collective goal notwithstanding possible negative implications for the minority.

Writing in 1863 John Stuart Mill described the utilitarian principle in his essay on the subject setting the highest standards of expected assessment of the pros and cons of a particular moral stance, including the need to address matters of quality as well as quantity. He offered something of an elitist version of utilitarianism that avoided the dangers of the democratic herd.

According to the Greatest Happiness Principle, as above explained, the ultimate end, with reference to and for the sake of which all other things are desirable (whether we are considering our own good or that of other people), is an existence exempt as far as possible from pain, and as rich as possible in enjoyments, both in point of quantity and quality; the test of quality, and the rule for measuring it against quantity, being the preference felt by those who in their opportunities of experience, to which must be added their habits of self-consciousness and self- observation, are best furnished with the means of comparison. This being, according to the utilitarian opinion, the end of human action, is necessarily also the standard of morality; which may accordingly be defined, the rules and precepts for human conduct, by the observance of which an existence such as has been described might be, to the greatest extent possible, secured to all mankind; and not to them only, but so far as the nature of things admits, to the whole sentient creation. (Mill, 1863/1992, p 123)

As described by Isaiah Berlin (1969) Mill's concept of happiness is rather more complex than Bentham's narrow focus.

Whatever happiness may be, it is, according to Mill, not what Bentham took it to be: for his conception of human nature is pronounced too narrow and altogether inadequate: he has no imaginative grasp of history or society or individual psychology; he does not understand either what holds, or what should hold, society together – common ideals, loyalties, national character; he is not aware of honour, dignity, self-culture, or the love of beauty, order, power, action; he understands only the 'business' aspects of life. Are these goals, which Mill rightly regards as central, so many means to a single universal goal – happiness? Or are they species of it? Mill never clearly tells us. He says that happiness – or utility – is of no use as a criterion of conduct – destroying at one blow the proudest claim, and indeed central doctrine of the Benthamite system. (Berlin, 1969, p xiv)

This lack of clarity of definition identified by Berlin is one of the principal difficulties with the utilitarian model.

Utilitarianism has been challenged as a system of calculation that potentially sacrifices individual needs and rights, and lets the floodgates open to majority oppression (Mill, 1859; Rawls, 1971; Heard, 1997). It has nevertheless retained a hold on moral discourse being viewed as a point of final arbitration in respect of cultural differences (Greene, 2014). However, John Gray (2014) has dismissed the utilitarian route to resolving conflicts as 'crude reductionism'. He discusses the difficulties of assessing happiness and wellbeing raised by Mill and offers this quote: 'It is better to be a human being dissatisfied, than a pig satisfied; better to be Socrates dissatisfied than a fool satisfied.' (Mill, 1863, p 14). The possibility of manufacturing happiness through cloning or psychological conditioning as posited in Huxley's *Brave New World* (1932) is flagged up as a further danger. Gray considers that the fluid and culture related nature of happiness defies a utilitarian cost benefit analysis.

Levenstein (2013) has endeavoured a synthesis in this dispute, albeit that his proposition is limited. He has identified the two core oppositional themes in moral philosophy as 'deontology', which considers that the moral content of an act derives from its adherence to a fixed rule independent of the consequences, and 'consequentialism', which accords the outcomes of an action as determining its moral worth. Discussing this tension principally in terms of the divergent pulls between individual human rights and collective utilitarianism, Levenstein argues for a pragmatic balancing of the two in respect of different aspects of public policy concerned with resource distribution in order to sustain human flourishing.

Marxism

For Marx, culture really has only one parent, and that is labour – which for him is equivalent to saying, exploitation. The culture of class society tends to repress this unwelcome truth; it prefers to dream up for itself a nobler progenitor, denying its lowly parenthood and imagining that it sprang simply from previous culture, or from the unfettered individual imagination. But Marx is out to remind us that our thought, like our very physical senses, is itself a product of the history with which it engages. History – the real world – always in some way outruns the thought which seeks to enfold it, and Marx, who as a good dialectician emphasises the dynamic, open-ended, interactive nature of things, detested those overweening systems of thought which (like Hegelian Idealism) believed that they could somehow stitch up the whole world within their concepts. It is darkly ironic that his own work would, among other things, give birth in time to just such sterile system-building. (Eagleton, 2001, p 271)

Marx's view of Idealist philosophy is an original one: he sees it as a form of fantasy, striving to attain in the mind what cannot yet be achieved in historical reality. And in this sense, the resolution of historical contradictions would spell the death of philosophical speculation. (Eagleton, 2001, p 277)

Marxism – one of the most dominant interpretations of social relations in the 20th century – sits somewhat uncomfortably in a discussion of moral philosophy argued in terms of elaborate theoretical constructs for human behaviour. Marxist materialism stands in contrast to the German idealism that had dominated philosophical thinking in the 19th century. Marxist interpretation of philosophical thought is one where, along with the entire cultural superstructure, philosophy is grounded in material relations – the operation of labour and the exploitation thereof (Eagleton, 2001).

> In the social production of their life, men enter into definite relations that are indispensable and independent of their will, *relations of production*, which correspond to a definite stage of development of their material productive *forces*. The sum total of these relations of production constitutes the economic structure of society, the real foundation, on which rises a legal and political superstructure and to which correspond definite forms of social consciousness. The mode of production of material life conditions the social, political and intellectual life process in general. It is not the consciousness of men that determines their being, but on the contrary, their social being that determines their consciousness. (Marx and Engels, 1859/1968, p 182, emphasis in original)

Marx does, however, see the potential of man as creator. Given the right material conditions following liberation from exploitation, debilitating, unmet physical needs and the grind of excessive work – creativity would flourish. Historical development would replace the class ridden exploitation dynamic of capitalism with a society free of the determining effects of private property; as a consequence the whole, balanced man would emerge capable of creativity and fulfilment. To this extent at least the morality of Marx is patently in evidence – a morality that promotes fulfilment in the tradition of Aristotle, the originator of one of the core strands of moral philosophy. The notion of realising the full human potential and achieving satisfaction thereby is clearly recognisable across these two giants of western philosophical thought. For both the establishment of the circumstances where such flourishing is most likely to occur is critical. The different approach of Marxism in this regard is one of expectation that such a conducive environment will evolve through a process of historical development at the interface between humanity and its relationship to the processes of production and associated power relations.

At the level of commanding particular behaviours Marx has little truck with morality assigning it to the role of a tool for class domination and a construct of justification for a particular set of social relations. In *The German Ideology* written in 1845/46 he offers a significant conception of ideas across philosophy, the arts and indeed the totality of culture as being the product of and dominated by a ubiquitous ruling class. He did not endorse the prompts to morality associated with the duty, utility, self-interest and moral sense discourse of moral philosophy (Eagleton, 2001; Malik, 2014).

> The ideas of the ruling class are in every epoch the ruling ideas, i.e. the class which is the ruling *material* force of society, is at the same time its ruling *intellectual* force. The class which has the means of material production at its disposal, has control at the same time over the means of mental production, so that thereby, generally speaking, the ideas of those who lack the means of mental production are subject to it. The ruling ideas are nothing more than the ideal expression of the dominant material relationships ... (Marx and Engels, 1845–46/1974, p 64, emphasis in original)

And yet for all the dismissal of both the world of ideas and moral precepts as froth atop a material existential reality, Marx himself engages in an intellectual critique and projection that acknowledges by the very commitment of his faculties to it a degree of human creative independence and capacity for worthwhile reflection. In terms of morality Marx's language and anticipation of historical development suggests a moral aspiration towards the fulfilled human being operating creatively with an absence of conflicted power relations. Malik notes that the language utilised in Marx's discourse belies any notion of detachment from a moral perspective with the operation of the historical phase of capitalism and a dominating bourgeois class described in value laden phrases and words such as:

> condemning 'robbery', 'slavery', 'suffering' and 'subjugation', describing capitalism as 'exploitation', 'brutalisation' and 'inhuman', and celebrating 'freedom'. (Malik, 2014, pp 231–2)

Certainly the revolutions and striving towards a utopian model of post capitalism which produced the communist states of the Soviet era was dominated by a strong moral philosophical tone abjuring inequality. In the event the political rush by the followers of Marx to model a new set of power relations owed much to utilitarianism with the interests of the majority promoted without heed to the rights of minorities. A version of utilitarianism was implemented which contrasted with Marx's specific rejection of morality grounded in utility. The aspiration of the communist states of the 20th century to establish utopian states also ran contrary to the Marxist approach of analysing the reality of the operation of material relations. (Eagleton, 2001; Malik, 2014)

Human rights

Human rights definition

Defining human rights is a contentious business, but the following definition suggested by Nickel in 1992 provides a plausible starting point.

> basic moral guarantees that people in all countries and cultures allegedly have simply because they are people. Calling these guarantees "rights" suggests that they attach to particular individuals who can invoke them, that they are of high priority, and that compliance with them is mandatory rather than discretionary. Human rights are frequently held to be universal in the sense that all people have and should enjoy them, and to be independent in the sense that they exist and are available as standards of justification and criticism whether or not they are recognized and implemented by the legal system or officials of a country. (Nickel, 1992, pp 561–2)

With the demise of the communist political world, Marxism has taken a back seat in philosophical debate – and in the morality stakes. What then is the current leading formulation of moral philosophical thought in the practical day-to-day operation of human relations? Religious edict as we have seen holds significant sway, but within secularism, and indeed pervading some aspects of religious morality, is the concept of human rights. Human rights comprise individual entitlements across multiple levels of human interaction, principally vis-à-vis the curtailment of oppressive power and domination. Expressed as accruing to the individual as potential 'victim', they have major implications for the behaviour of individuals operating solo and as part of group operations – society.

The significance of human rights for the 21st century is that they are providing something akin to a global point of behavioural reference spilling over into international justice systems. They are a political reality that demand by their frequent incantation acknowledgement in a discussion of moral philosophy.

Despite prominence in the 20th and 21st centuries, human rights as a concept is by no means new – rather it has been subject to evolutionary thought and has taken different guises. These variations of interpretation have largely been associated with scale of application, for example whether rights only encompass civil rights – freedom from oppression – or whether they also embrace social rights – entitlement to the means to life and fulfilment. Rights are also inflationary being capable of an expanding interpretation in response to the interests of particular social groups, usually identified in terms of disadvantage or vulnerability, for example women and children.

Philosophic grounding

In terms of philosophic grounding numerous philosophers have had an input into the human rights canon. John Locke has been identified as one of the earliest protagonists of human rights – or, as he described them, natural rights. Locke considered that humans in their state of nature prior to the formation of society were in possession of natural rights such as the rights to life, liberty and property. Locke's *Second Treatise on Government* (1690) discussed the role of these rights in prompting societal development. Governments were established for the purpose of their protection and consequently governmental power was restricted; it did not lay claim to the rights themselves, which continued to rest with the individual. This 'classical liberalism' made a significant contribution to the redefinition of the relationship between government and citizens, shifting presumptions away from absolute monarchy towards government accountability (The Levin Institute, The State University of New York, 2015).

Thomas Paine developed a polemic on similar lines. An 18th-century philosopher and commentator, Paine had a high political profile with links to the American and French revolutions. Continuing the argument in support of the concept of natural rights in *Rights of Man* (1791), Paine discussed the transference of natural rights to the civil domain, and the retention of rights by the individual in the context of civil power. His contention was that people retain natural rights and consequently the population has sovereignty in respect of the governance instituted to protect their rights (Philp, 2013).

In his analysis of the philosophical grounding of human rights, the former United States Ambassador to the United Nations Commission on Human Rights, Jerome Shestack, cited Kant's conception of the paramount role of the individual having responsibility for his/her actions as a free and rational agent.

> Rights then flow from the autonomy of the individual in choosing his or her ends, consistent with a similar freedom for all.
>
> In short, Kant's great imperative is that the central focus of morality is personhood, namely the capacity to take responsibility as a free and rational agent for one's system of ends. A natural corollary of this Kantian thesis is that the highest purpose of human life is to will autonomously. A person must always be treated as an end, and the highest purpose of the state is to promote conditions favouring the free and harmonious unfolding of individuality. (Shestack, 1998, p 216)

This is a justification for civil rights – freedom from oppression. Shestack then proceeded to examine what are in effect social rights – the justification of aspiration to equality in Rawls' *Theory of Justice*. From behind the 'veil of ignorance' Rawls had suggested that two principles would emerge; in addition to the primary one associated with civil liberties such as freedom of person, speech, conscience and politics, Rawls identified the importance of equality and fairness.

> Social and economic inequalities are to be arranged so that they are both: (a) to the greatest benefit of the least advantaged, consistent with the just savings principle, and (b) attached to offices and positions open to all under conditions of fair equality of opportunity. (Rawls, 1971, p 302)

Rawls considered that rights founded on this justice to be inviolable.

> Each person possesses an inviolability founded on justice that even the welfare of society as a whole cannot override. (Rawls, 1971, p 3)

Development in the political arena

On the political front, the beginnings of human rights as an idea can be traced through a series of formal declarations. Explorations of the origins of human rights frequently make reference to a sixth century BC record of the conquest of Babylon in 539 BC by Cyprus the Great, a Persian king. Inscribed on a clay cylinder is a set of humane precepts by which Cyprus proposed to govern. However far he may have fallen short on delivery, the declaration has formed a point of reference for the development of the concept of human rights in antiquity. It is in effect a charter, which the United Nations has endorsed as an example of the early formulation of universal rights.

> I announce that I will respect the traditions, customs and religions of the nations of my empire and never let any of my governors and subordinates look down on or insult them until I am alive. From now on, till God grants me the kingdom favor, I will impose my monarchy on no nation. Each is free to accept it, and if any one of them rejects it, I never resolve on war to reign. Until I am the king of Persia, Babylon, and the nations of the four directions, I never let anyone oppress any others, and if it occurs, I will take his or her right back and penalize the oppressor. ...
>
> And until I am the monarch, I will never let anyone take possession of movable and landed properties of the others by force or without compensation. Until I am alive, I prevent unpaid, forced labor. To day, I announce that everyone is free to choose a religion. People are free to live in all regions and take up a job provided that they never violate other's rights. ...
>
> No one could be penalised for his or her relatives' faults. I prevent slavery and my governors and subordinates are obliged to prohibit exchanging men and women as slaves within their own ruling domains. Such a traditions should be exterminated the world over. (cited in Nice, 2014)

In the British tradition medieval Magna Carta is widely celebrated as a document establishing fundamental freedoms in opposition to over weaning, unchecked and arbitrary governance. In the tug of war between monarch, in this instance King John I, and the aristocracy, the Magna Carta was a statement of freedom that ultimately came to form the basis of protection of all individuals. It included the celebrated right of habeas corpus (Nice, 2014).

The principles of natural rights developed by Locke (1690) were in evidence in two revolutionary political movements in the 18th century – in the breaking away of the United States from the United Kingdom and in the overthrow of an oppressive old guard European regime in France. They are iterated in the United States in its Declaration of Independence and in France in its Declaration of the Rights of Man and of the Citizen.

United States: Declaration of Independence (1776)

We hold these truths to be self-evident, that all men are created equal, that they are endowed by their Creator with certain unalienable Rights, that among these are Life, Liberty and the pursuit of Happiness.--That to secure these rights, Governments are instituted among Men, deriving their just powers from the consent of the governed, --That whenever any Form of Government becomes destructive of these ends, it is the Right of the People to alter or to abolish it, and to institute new Government, laying its foundation on such principles and organizing its powers in such form, as to them shall seem most likely to effect their Safety and Happiness. (United States Congress, 1776)

France: Declaration of the Rights of Man and of the Citizen (1789)

The representatives of the French people, organised as a National Assembly, believing that the ignorance, neglect, or contempt of the rights of man are the sole cause of public calamities and of the corruption of governments, have determined to set forth in a solemn declaration the natural, unalienable, and sacred rights of man, in order that this declaration, being constantly before all the members of the Social body, shall remind them continually of their rights and duties; in order that the acts of the legislative power, as well as those of the executive power, may be compared at any moment with the objects and purposes of all political institutions and may thus be more respected, and, lastly, in order that the grievances of the citizens, based hereafter upon simple and incontestable principles, shall tend to the maintenance of the constitution and redound to the happiness of all.

Article first. Men are born and remain free and equal in rights. Social distinctions may be based only on considerations of the common good.

Article 2. The aim of every political association is the preservation of the natural and imprescriptible rights of Man. These rights are Liberty, Property, Safety and Resistance to Oppression. (National Assembly of France, 1789)

In the 20th century declarations of human rights have followed the horrors of their erosion and the abuse of institutional power during the Second World War. The United Nations adopted the Universal Declaration of Human Rights in 1948 opening as follows.

> Whereas recognition of the inherent dignity and of the equal and inalienable rights of all members of the human family is the foundation of freedom, justice and peace in the world.
> Article 1. All human beings are born free and equal in dignity. They are endowed with reason and conscience and should act toward one another in a spirit of brotherhood. (United Nations General Assembly, 1948)

The declaration encompasses a breadth of interactions addressing the rights between individuals and in respect of groups across civil rights and social, economic and cultural rights. Multiple human rights international justice procedures have followed this declaration and there has been engagement with enforcement through international law. Conventions have been held and domestic legislation enacted. Within Europe the 1954 European Convention on Human Rights with its own series of articles enabled individuals to petition directly to Europe in respect of violations (Nice, 2014).

Alongside statements of necessary universal liberties, social rights have acquired a high profile in 20th and 21st century political discourse on human rights. The interrelationship between freedoms and entitlements has become increasingly apparent in a social environment that sets high expectations of state intervention in the interests of promoting the welfare of citizens. For example, attaining essential living standards has an obvious link with the right to freedom from inhuman and degrading treatment, and there are many other associations between civil and social rights that render the division between the two types of rights somewhat anachronistic in the eyes of some commentators.

Abandoning the conventional dichotomy can give us a clearer picture of the nature and range of human rights and allow us to see much more clearly their manifold interrelationships. Our lives – and the rights we need to live them with dignity – do not fall into largely separate political and socioeconomic spheres. (Donnelly, 2003, p 32)

Human rights aim to identify both the necessary negative and positive prerequisites for leading a minimally good life, such as rights against torture and rights to health care. This aspiration has been enshrined in various declarations and legal conventions issued during the past 50 years, initiated by the Universal Declaration of Human Rights (1948) and perpetuated by, most importantly, the European Convention on Human Rights (1954) and the International Covenant on Civil and Economic Rights (1966). Together these three documents form the centrepiece of a moral doctrine that many consider to be capable of providing the contemporary geo-political order with what amounts to an international bill of rights. However, the doctrine of human rights does not aim to be a fully comprehensive moral doctrine. An appeal to human rights does not provide us with a fully comprehensive account of morality per se. Human rights do not, for example, provide us with criteria for answering such questions as whether telling lies is inherently immoral, or what the extent of one's moral obligations to friends and lovers ought to be? What human rights do primarily aim to identify is the basis for determining the shape, content, and scope of fundamental, public moral norms. (Fagan, 2015)

This summary of the role of human rights identifies their substantial current influence alongside their limitations. It indicates their particular reference to the public rather than the private sphere – in effect the interface between morality and public policy.

Moral complexity

The sheer multiplicity of developments within rationalist moral philosophy – in addition to revelatory traditions – presents endeavours to simplify understanding of the human condition and thereby manage morality with colossal barriers. As we have seen from this resume, there are major divergences both in the interpretation of behaviour and in conceiving the aspiration and construction of morality. As a consequence any search for commonality as the means for grappling with complex moral thought faces not a little difficulty.

Commonality

These examples across revelatory morality and the secular rationalist arguments of moral philosophers are expositions of perspectives that prima facie are exclusive; while there are strands of conceptual overlap, by and large they are not in the business of 'commonality'. Even the attempt to establish a mediating principle of utilitarianism in respect of differences in morality is based on the presumption that this particular approach offers a superior model of morality with the potential for universal application.

There is, however, a discourse that does endeavour to tease out the elements of commonality between moralities – to seek a common point of reference and even an explanation of the phenomenon. This strain of thought is not new; it stretches across the span of western philosophy and tradition. Socratic thought pre-supposed a common moral universe, a common positive within which rational debate could operate and result in agreement. In this thesis humanity is viewed as having a common motivation with irreconcilable stances being due to lack of understanding or misconception. Descartes (1641) and Leibniz (1710) offered an underlying root cause explanatory unifier. Their philosophic approach viewed a pro-social stance as consequent on self-interested rational calculation. In contrast, a major thread of commonality in the interpretation of morality has veered away from rational interest towards the emotion of empathy. In the 18th century, David Hume in his *Treatise on Human Nature* viewed natural sympathy as the overriding influence on the derivation of morality.

> We may observe that all the circumstances requisite for its [sympathy's] operation are found in most of the virtues; which have, for the most part, a tendency to the good of society, or to that of the person possessed of them. If we compare all these circumstances, we shall not doubt, that sympathy is the chief source of moral distinctions; especially when we reflect, that no objection can be raised against this hypothesis in one case, which will not extend to all cases. Justice is certainly approved of for no other reason, than because it has a tendency to the public good; and the public good is indifferent to us, except so far as sympathy

interests us in it. We may presume the like with regard to all the other virtues, which have a like tendency to the public good. They must derive all their merit from our sympathy with those, who reap any advantage from them; as the virtues, which have a tendency to the good of the person possessed of them, derive their merit from our sympathy with him. (Hume, 1738/1888, p 618)

More recently Darwin has been credited with being one of the most prominent advocates of instinctive empathy as the core explanatory motive for morality, an emotion he associated with the parent child relationship.

… any animal whatever, endowed with well-marked social instincts, the parental and filial affections being here included, would inevitably acquire a moral sense or conscience, as soon as its intellectual powers had become as well, or nearly as well developed as in man. (Darwin, 1871, pp 71–2)

A pro-social commonality supported by the empathetic emotions and/ or rationality is a recurrent, though varied, theme. It is an optimistic model that has much in common with enlightenment convictions of 'progress' and even deterministic interpretations of the operation of society that have an expectation that moral behaviour will flourish in the correct social environment and that moral behaviour can be explained by socioeconomic circumstance – Marxism being the example par excellence.

There are, however, major challenges to this conception of a humanity motivated by common pro-social values. A tranche of thinking has been pre-occupied with other motives rather less associated with empathy – single, all-encompassing drives such as Freud's interpretation of the role of sex and latterly, more negatively, his identification of a congruent motive – an underlying death wish (Freud, 1905; 1920). Hobbes (1651), Nietzsche (1886), Adler (1929) and others considered that the determining motive was the aspiration for power. Empathy is squeezed from these scenarios with selfish, single motive undercurrents providing an explanation for the not inconsiderable variety of human relationships and actions.

Relativism

Somewhat in contrast to advocates of commonality in morality have been exponents of divergence. 'Relativism' is often associated with liberalism and the endorsement of a tolerant society with no standards or commonly identified motives for morality – simply a laissez faire response to a host of ideas. The endorsement of tolerance and avoidance of oppression is the purpose of John Stuart Mill's commitment to this approach in *On Liberty* (1859). Strawson is similarly concerned to promote fairness catering for different sorts of people and to provide an environment that would spark new thoughts and ideas. His principal argument favouring pluralism, however, relates to the impossibility of reconciling ideas and perspectives.

> The region of the ethical is the region where there are truths but no truth... (Strawson, 1974, p 28–9)

He discusses the tension between Bertrand Russell and D.H. Lawrence with their irreconcilable views of man:

> It would be absurd to hope for a reconciliation of the two conflicting attitudes. It is not absurd to desire that both should exist in conflict. (Strawson, 1974, p 44)

Relativism has become pervasive in the 20th and 21st centuries because of three associated developments. Firstly, there has been a reaction to the rigidity of moral codes, a growing individualism – of which Sartre's existentialism is an example. Secondly, there is considerable recent evidence of shifts in moral precepts over time, for example norms associated with gender relations and sexuality. And thirdly there is an increased understanding of the differences between cultures as revealed in anthropological studies alongside a demand for liberalism associated with multicultural living. These issues are considered in greater length in Chapter Three.

Simultaneously, however, there has been a reaction against unbridled relativism. The difficulty in managing a society with no point of connection or reference for moral standards has been widely noted, particularly in the context of the sponsorship of multiculturalism (Henricson, 2012). Mary Midgley, while eschewing total solution approaches, endorses the need to find some point of commonality:

Pluralism is quite right to insist that we must abandon the wild ambitions of unbridled system-builders, but that does not mean it must land us with an irreducible plurality of totally disconnected human aims instead. (Midgley, 1984, p 26)

A scientific perspective

The current multiple pressures supporting a relativistic perspective in assessing morality are balanced to a degree by the application of scientific investigations that by their nature presuppose an element of commonality. Obviously there is an historical continuum of investigation; consideration of human behaviour has been evident in literature, religion, law and most aspects of conscious living from time immemorial. More recently, however, there have been some highly significant and distinctive developments that draw on what might be described as the scientific method. This analysis involves naturalistic observations, psychological analyses of human impulses and neurological investigations into the operation of the brain and behaviours. Darwin provided the initial impetus for this approach in *The Descent of Man* (1871) leading the way with naturalistic observations and an emergent theory of evolution that had major implications for understanding morality.

Darwin's thinking and observations encompassed the full range of human instincts and their intrinsic tensions. But, concurring with Hume, he considered empathy – the social instincts – to be the prime determinant of morality. Darwin reflected on the multiple impulses and instincts with the combined capacity for memory, intelligent thought and language that typify humanity. His conclusion was that morality would have arisen in any species with comparable intellectual capacities, and that it was the result of a need to order and prioritise impulses so as to avoid regret over succumbing to one at the expense of another. This process through language and social exchange had become not only an internal cognitive function but was also externalised in the form of codes across groups.

Darwin recognised the complexity of motives, impulses and habit that determine human action. The array of instincts, needs and behaviours were described from hunger, to shame and fear of approbation, to the parent child relationship. His understanding of the web of mood, motive, and cultural and biological influences on conduct was considerable, and links were drawn with other species. He nevertheless focused on two principal drivers – the social instincts and innate aggression, and deemed the social instincts to be prioritised within morality because they provide longer-term satisfaction.

> ... as soon as the mental faculties had become highly developed, images of all past actions and motives would be incessantly passing through the brain of each individual: and that feeling of dissatisfaction, or even misery, which invariably results, as we shall hereafter see, from any unsatisfied instinct, would arise, as often as it was perceived that the enduring and always present social instinct had yielded to some other instinct, at the time stronger, but neither enduring in its nature, nor leaving behind it a very vivid impression. It is clear that many instinctive desires, such as that of hunger, are in their nature of short duration; and after being satisfied, are not readily or vividly recalled. (Darwin, 1871, p 72)

Darwin's findings concerning evolutionary psychology and the processes of moral behaviour have been complemented in more recent developments. Neuroimaging or brain scanning have found the location of pro-social emotions such as compassion, gratitude, pride, shame, regret and guilt in the ventromedial prefrontal cortex. (Moll and de Oliveira-Souze, 2007). Through a combination of neuroscience and psychological experimentation, a powerful process of unconscious decision-making has been identified (e.g. Haidt, 2001; Hauser, 2006). Responses are often immediate, intuitive and strongly linked to the emotive, and, where reasoning is deployed to explain decisions, it has been found to be predominantly the result of subsequent rationalisation (Haidt, 2007, 2012).

We have become aware of a strong role for features in the brain concerned with emotions, but it is not the exclusive domain with influence. Cognitive ordering of decisions also features, as it does in Darwin's discourse on empathy and the control of behaviour. Although psychological research has demonstrated the intuitive and habitual nature of immediate responses on moral issues, there is also evidence that when further in depth consideration is given there is an ability to analyse and as a consequence to readjust those initial positions (Greene, 2014). The role of the brain's prefrontal cortex in hosting cognition has also been identified; it has a function in guiding and ordering thought and actions, in relating past to future and in formulating and executing goals involving a capacity to consider the benefits to be secured in the longer term (Fuster et al, 2000; Shimamura, 2000; Miller et al, 2002).

However, while a dual role for emotion and cognitive order have been established, the way in which these impulses interact within the individual is not fully understood and critically not to the degree of rendering behaviour predictable. The interplay of a plethora of emotions and the role and capacity of cognitive faculties in reality to marshal order is subject to question. Certainly the nature of the prioritisation being sought does not appear to be pre-determined across the species.

A significant point of fluidity relates to the element of difference in genetic make-up within a given population. This fraught issue is compounded by a social evolution construction floated by some psychologists who have attributed differences to the need for societies to have a spread of dispositions for sustained survival (Haidt, 2001; Tuschman, 2013). The proposition is that, in terms of social functioning, it is important to have a population group with a proportion of individuals with a caring, sharing and trust orientation, on the one hand, balanced by a proportion of those with egocentric, go-getting and authoritarian leanings, on the other (Tuschman, 2013). Whether or not this social evolution interpretation of difference is plausible, what cannot be disputed is the difference that exists between individuals in terms of the operation of impulses. A major influence on that difference is undoubtedly the overlay of a multiplicity of cultural influences (Haidt, 2001, 2012). A simple observation of the span of divergence between morality in different cultural settings and in relation to cultural change over time is sufficient to underwrite such a role for culture as described Chapter Four.

These findings associated with the brain, the genes and the impact of culture give rise to the difficult and highly controversial question as to how much of human behaviour is pre-determined and how much is genuine discretion in moral choices. The challenge of this limitation of free will to ethics and the role of legal sanction has been widely noted (Harman, 1999; Doris, 2002; Greene, 2003).

The benefits and dangers of scientific endeavour

The accumulation of scientific evidence and understanding of the operation of the brain, behaviours, dispositions and motives is undoubtedly highly pertinent to the management of morality. It offers the possibility of policy responses being fine-tuned to individual and collective thought processes and conduct. Bentham's utilitarianism, Kant's deontology and also to a degree Aristotle's value ethics, place a premium on rational thought. The reason for this is that these philosophies are in the game of pronouncing on how humans should conduct their decisions rather than responding to how in fact they do so. The point needs to be made that in establishing an aspiration there are benefits to be had from understanding how in reality decisions are made and what the determinants of human behaviour are – the world of scientific observation.

It is also worthy of note that there are benefits to be had from scientific endeavour in terms of interventions where these can be supportive. The reparation of brain damage and therapeutic tools to assuage psychological distortion and distress can enhance wellbeing. There is, however, a tip over point, albeit ill defined, between support and manipulation, and with the availability of pharmaceutical and psychological interventions, the understanding of the human 'soul' is fraught with danger. The threat ranges from within individual psychiatric care to population 'nudging'. The lack of easily defined boundaries renders guarding against the dangers highly problematic for responsible governance. This is a risk that is beginning to be recognised and studies are being conducted on the ethical dimension of advances in neuroscience, for example by the Oxford Centre for Neuroethics.

Overview

This chapter has juxtaposed and commented on the major aspects of current trends in morality – the scope of morality, its sources and the understanding of its purpose and functioning. There has been consideration of revelatory religion and the revelation rational split that has fuelled the religious secular divide. Within rationalism we have had an assessment of approaches endorsing individual and collective fulfilment, virtue ethics, deontology and duty, the outcomes stance of utilitarianism, Marxist materialism, human rights through to the plurality of relativism. There has been an examination of the association between the emotional and cognitive aspects of the brain and the modus operandi of human behaviour including synergies and divergence on the intermeshed fronts of biology and culture. The breadth of morality across the gamut of life has become apparent from the discussion, as has the persistence of difference in perspectives and interpretation, alongside outstanding gaps in knowledge.

We have seen the significance of the centrifugal pulls between key contemporaneous moral perspectives. They have multiple implications for public policy and constitute the core issues to be considered when the state is managing morality and responding to moral precepts. They have implications when it comes to decisions about whether or not to support the status quo, and they have a bearing on how to address attitudinal divergence and change within society.

The desire for universal answers – commonality within morality – has become strong in the search for a sense of security in a world with shifting sands of uncertain belief. But the dominion of desire over facts needs to be resisted. Scientific models have offered something of a commonality solution, but the evidence of relativism still pertains. There has perhaps been too much reliance on the solutions of biology displacing the fluidity of culture. There are questions to be posed, too, about the nature of biological interpretation – the interplay and the questionable elevation of empathy at the expense of other impulses within motivation. Relativism and the role of culture in diversity are particularly evident in the split between revelatory and rational derivations of morality. But even that split is not clear-cut. The colours run into each other and there are overlays of influences that permeate the divide. Simple solutions whether in unity or dichotomy are simply not to hand. It is the complexity and the missing pieces with which we must grapple; further investigation on these lines is undertaken in the next chapter.

THREE

Synergies and tensions: morality as an accommodation of human impulses in different cultural contexts

In the last chapter we examined broad, divergent moral perspectives with potential implications for public policy. The likelihood of strains emerging in conjoining such a disparate set of approaches to living is self-evident, and yet that is the requirement in a modern pluralistic society. In order to develop an enhanced and inclusive model for the societal and public administrative interface with morality it is necessary to probe and contextualise the interrelationship between these strands of thought, their synergy and tensions, and the degree to which they require accommodation; that is the purpose of this chapter.

Consideration is given to the elements of commonality in morality, the characteristics of those elements and their legitimacy in terms of potential to underwrite a framework for the management of morality. The apparent contradiction posed by relativism – expectations of and acquiescence in differences with no common point of reference – is reviewed in the context of the conclusion reached on the question of commonality.

The split between revelatory approaches to morality and those developed in a secular context is undoubtedly problematic in the accommodation stakes. Examples of the impact of that split are cited to assess the scale of the challenge for public policy. There is investigation of the role, overlap and potential for coexistence of these two strands of thinking in the weave of 21st-century culture, including their parameters and relationship to the law. The overarching influence of 'tribalism' is also considered.

Commonality and empathy

The emphasis on empathy by Darwin and others as the primary emotion underwriting morality offers a prima facie common platform for the development of a cohesive public policy on morality. Some of the findings of neuroscience demonstrating the location of social instincts in the brain have lent further credence to the empathy thesis. However, examination in a broader context suggests that the relationship between morality and the emotions is considerably more fluid and complex than this, with a rather more dominant role for other impulses and layered and divergent cultural influences.

Questioning empathy as the sole harbinger of long-term satisfaction

Much credit has been given to Darwin's view that morality is the mechanism by which empathy is prioritised in human conduct. The view is that it enables humans to manage fleeting and contradictory impulses that run counter to pro-social behaviour. But is this really so? Is it sufficiently resonant with the evidence of moral codes and practice?

There is a range of unanswered questions and issues pursuant to Darwin's proposition. The principal one of these relates to his contention that the longer-term satisfaction offered by the social instincts lies at the root of their superior ranking within morality. While both the longer-term and profound nature of the good and meaningful life may be widely endorsed and the benefits of an element of deferred gratification recognised, the prioritisation of the social instincts within the framework of moral philosophy is by no means a given.

Gratification that satisfies the ego in ways not necessarily to do with social instincts may be pursued as a long-term goal, for example in relation to sustaining interests of the mind, the pursuit of arts and the acquisition of status symbols. Then there is the assuagement of hunger through long-term forward planning. Critically there is the fulfilment of the emotional drives of the ego in relation to sexuality which can involve sustained action contravening the social mores of the group: homosexuality, adultery and desertion.

These and many other examples can be given of the pursuit of the meaningful life that involves a considered prioritisation of aspects of the ego that are not to do with social instincts. The fulfilment of other needs can produce long-term satisfaction, and if denied can result in emotional, intellectual or physical crippling. Indeed it has been the denial of these egoistical needs that has caused some thinkers to deprecate rigid codes of conduct in favour of a liberated ego.

Morality holds the reins for multiple emotions

The evidence suggests that it is questionable whether the social instincts are necessarily the prime purpose of morality. Might not morality be the management of different emotional and cognitive pulls within the human psyche with the social instincts being one but not necessarily the dominant pull? Certainly the strength of other influences is incontrovertible. Darwin's own catalogue of human drivers across hunger, self-preservation, aggression and fear is witness to that, as are the arguments put forward by advocates of sex and power as principal determinants of human conduct. The contention in this discussion is that morality acts as an accommodator of this breadth of impulse. It encompasses far more than empathy, fellow feeling and the social instincts of caring.

Science has confirmed this interpretation grounding it in the intricate workings of the brain and observation of the complexity of human behaviour across cultures. In these findings of the operation of habit, cognition, emotion, what does not emerge is any clear thematic indication of a single route to prioritisation. Rather what is apparent are a host of impulses with different ones being prioritised at different times and in different circumstances, and frequently we see the operation of impulses in tandem unprioritised.

As profiled in the discussion of revelatory morality in Chapter Two, religions tend to recognise and embrace a breadth of impulses with life models that encompass egotism, the reinforcement of authority, social and sexual repression, violence and sadism, artistic fulfilment and more — as well as empathetic concern. In many cases the full breadth of living habits are addressed from sexual regulation to eating habits and medical practice. Religions frequently have an expectation of proselytising; the duty to persuade others to join a belief set is not infrequently taken to the extreme of physical violence. There are also examples across religions of ascetic reclusive habits being viewed as the zenith of moral of conduct — an impulse rather more concerned with eliminating the burden of choice and want than caring. There is the support for authority at the level of family through to the state, which is a major component of many moralities — a question principally to do with power relations. And closely linked with the bolstering of authority is the upholding of the status quo in respect of material matters, with theft deemed immoral notwithstanding gross inequalities.

Revelatory systems and the bolstering of authority – the example of Hinduism

Support for the caste system in Hinduism in India is one of the most overt examples of the religious trait of authoritarianism. The Hindu Vedas scriptures endorsed this stultifying hierarchical social structure. Initially four castes were established – brahmins (priests), kshatriya (aristocrats and warriors), vaishya (merchants and farmers) and shudra (labourers). Subsequently a lower order was introduced outside the caste system – the dalits (untouchables). Myths justifying the caste system became included in the Hindu religion's narrative as the caste system evolved to support a highly ordered social framework replacing a declining less rigid and localised clan structure. Social order was very much a primary function within Hinduism and, as the requirements of hierarchical control increased, so too did religious support for an expansion of the caste system differentiating details of work and social intercourse practice (Malik, 2014). Supporting a received orthodoxy is exemplified across religions. While Hinduism contains a highly elaborate and rigid mechanism, the expectation and pressures to accede to an established order is also the stuff of Christianity and Islam, notwithstanding concerns to redress the extremes of poverty.

Within secular morality, too, there is evidence of this wider accommodation of impulses. Hobbes writing in the 17th century, for example, saw human motivation as governed by appetites and aversions which social structures and morality were intended to manage to avoid the destruction of humankind by antagonistic, power driven individuals. Hobbes' social contract thesis clearly contrasts with a model driven by empathy. While it has been criticised for its exclusive negativity, few would deny that *Leviathan* contains recognisable elements of the human condition (Hobbes, 1651).

There is a more tempered perspective within secular moral philosophy that acknowledges the behavioural trait of weighing up options and divergent claims in the context of life's pressures in order to achieve a meaningful life without necessarily prioritising the social instincts. Bernard Williams is the leading exponent of this train of philosophical thought. In *Moral Luck* (1981) he chooses the example of the artist Gauguin to describe the process. In this instance the call of individual artistic fulfilment trumps adherence to social instincts, and this draws the approval of the community because of the product – great art. The barometer that Williams uses is one of avoiding the emotion of regret; it involves weighing up multiples of feelings, impulses, relationships, rules and outcomes – a minefield.

The concept of *fulfilment* has a history throughout the development of moral philosophy from the Ancient Greeks to the present; it can be traced through virtue ethics, utilitarianism, civil liberties and facilitating equality. Aristotle's good and meaningful life, intended to secure *eudaimonia*, translated as happiness or human flourishing, suggests an approach that is neutral on the question of the social instincts and rather more inclined to a goal of self-fulfilment.

Overall, taking both religious and secular morality into account, the evidence suggests that historically there have been moralities that offer recognition and accommodation to a spectrum of human traits. Morality it seems is associated with the interplay of a wide variety of needs including, for example, fear, egotism and even cruelty, alongside pro-social empathy.

The role of morality revealed by changes in moral perspectives over time

Shifts in morality – episodic change and movement over time – provide one of the clearest indications of morality as the tool endeavouring to hold the reins between muddled drivers of the human psyche. These include major shifts in sexual mores, intergenerational relations, filial duties, expectations of self-sacrifice and self-realisation, obedience and challenge to authority within the family, community and the state, and attitudes and behaviour towards the 'other'. These multiple and changing norms can be found in revelatory as well as secular systems of morality. Examples of their incidence are considered here.

Changes in sexual relations

Let us take sexual mores as a first example, an issue that pervades human life and is fraught. It would be plausible to make the case that moral precepts governing sexual relations have had the protection of children as their principal raison d'être. Within Christian doctrine there are requirements associated with enduring, close adult relationships between parents, namely marriage. In the UK, Christian morality in this sphere has largely been incorporated in law, but as other impulses besides the social instincts associated with child protection have sought to hold sway, we have not only witnessed the odd transgression of moral codes, but also a change in majority public attitudes. Attitudes towards single parenthood, cohabitees and divorce have become increasingly liberal. They no longer endorse the necessity of an intimate partnership for life, disparage illegitimacy and extra marital sex or oppose divorce. The British Social Attitudes Survey shows a rapidly increasing tolerance of pre-marital sex and of couples having children outside marriage during the close of the 20th century and the first decade of the 21st century (Barlow et al, 2001; Duncan and Phillips, 2008). Some 66 per cent of those interviewed supported the proposition that 'There is little difference between being married and living together' as against 19 per cent disagreeing (Duncan and Phillips, 2008). A similar percentage,

63 per cent, agreed with the statement that 'Divorce can be a positive first step towards a new life', while only 7 per cent disagreed (Barlow et al, 2008).

Reflecting public attitudes often belatedly and sometimes ahead of the groundswell of views, the law has changed over the 20th and 21st centuries. Divorce has become more readily available. There has also been a growing acceptance of the concept of the single adult carer with the removal of financial incentives to get married by the New Labour government; their reintroduction by the subsequent Coalition government has been widely criticised (Henricson, 2012). Within the Church of England itself there has been a slow erosion of hostility to change with marriages for divorcees now being conducted under its auspices.

These profound changes beg the question – why do we no longer feel that the economic and emotional protection of children needs to be met through the security offered by an enduring adult couple parental relationship? Are we talking here about material changes in today's society? Some such changes have indeed taken place; the ability of a single parent to survive economically has increased. Female employment and the welfare state have contributed to this element of liberation. Progress in and access to contraceptive methods in the 20th century, too, has facilitated smaller, more manageable families. However, there are also countervailing factors. In a world where relative poverty takes a serious toll on the wellbeing of both adults and children (Wilkinson and Marmot, 2003; Commission on Families and the Wellbeing of Children, 2005), the risk for the child of a single parent of encountering poverty is considerably greater than for the child of a together couple (Eurostat, 2011). Furthermore, while families may produce fewer children, the period of their financial dependency has substantially increased. We have moved from the child labour of the Dickensian era through to the introduction of compulsory schooling with the obligatory school leaving age now standing at 18 years, and expectations that young people will undergo further education. The economic arguments point to the benefits accruing to the young of having two parents living together able to shoulder the provision of this level of financial support to their offspring. For the single parent household, the obligation on the absent parent to pay maintenance is of limited compensation because of the cost of running two households.

In terms of providing material support to children there are no arguments favouring the loosening of the obligations to marry. But what about the emotional front? While aggressive, violent adult relationships have a detrimental impact on children's wellbeing (Chase-Lansdale and Hetherington, 1990; Richards, 1993), the evidence supports the argument that children brought up by parents in a non-violent couple relationship benefit in terms of behavioural outcomes compared with children in lone parent families (Bynner, 2001; Gerard and Buehler, 2004). The evidence is also unambiguous on the detrimental impact on children's welfare of separation and divorce.

> There is evidence to show that, not only do young people experience a two-year adjustment crisis period (Demo and Aycock, 1988), they also suffer disproportionately from health, social and educational problems, particularly if subject to repeated disruptions (Pryor and Rodgers, 2001). (Commission on Families and the Wellbeing of Children, 2005, p 23)

In their summary of the family risk factors for children for the Department for Education, Jones, Gutman and Platt (2013) found that lone parenthood carried with it high risks on both the material and emotional front:

> Lone parenthood is associated with high risks of family poverty, which is itself widely recognised as being associated with worse outcomes for children at different ages and on a range of measures (Ermisch, 2009; Sabates and Dex, 2012; Washbrook, 2010). Lone parenthood may also represent a 'risk' because one parent is necessarily constrained in the amount of activities that she or he can carry out with a child, whereas two parents can offer greater flexibility and share parenting and caring roles. In addition, lone parenthood has been found to be a risk factor through the disruption and family stress that is typically associated with the breakdown of a relationship. (Jones, Gutman and Platt, 2013, pp 35–6)

The pointers suggest that in the case of adult couple relationships moral change has not been prompted by the social instincts. Rather they suggest that other impulses have held increasing sway including the quest for sexual fulfilment and what has been described as the narcissistic pleasure of being in love. Romantic love as a cultural product of 19th- and 20th-century inflation of the significance of human sensibilities has to a degree taken hold and acquired licence in an era when individuality and individual fulfilment are at a premium (Duncan and Phillips, 2008).

Changes in attitudes to authority

The second example of moral change relates to another level of social relations – the decline in deference and the challenge to authority. There is an argument to be made that the social instincts have a contributory role to play in the elaborate edifice that constitutes authority within societies of relatively small scale through to complex ones of the dimensions of the UK. For a society to hold together there is the necessity for order; and for that order to be maintained authority is needed throughout interconnected social relationships from the family to criminal justice to market operations, public services, administration, government and more. Morality, particularly as evoked by received institutions such as the established church and the law, has been concerned with upholding that authority.

The social benefits of so doing – facilitating day-to-day living, security, social functioning and forward planning – tie this process in with the social instincts. Although there may be some distance between the emotion of empathy and the theoretical intricacies of the law, the case can be made that there is a connection. However, there are also other influences and impulses involved in bolstering authority. Key amongst these is the whole conglomeration of power relations. They include dominance in sexual relations (predominantly men over women), across generations (movement in and out of power across the age span), market muscle, wealth accumulation and the control of resources. The impulses at play involve aggression, greed, interpersonal dominance, power, submission, fear and loyalty. There are examples of the social instincts being engaged, but they do not predominate in the impulse web associated with the imposition of authority. Neither do they in its challenge.

Authority is historically the subject of challenge. While some societies exhibit a relative calm, these are in the minority. The Marxist trajectory, with its materialist perspective on human relations, sees a movement of authority in tandem with changes to the means of production (Marx and Engels, 1975/2005). Few would question that dynamic – though most would not endorse Marxism's dictatorship of the proletariat as the final point of determination and resolution; rather the unrest of the individual and the group is likely, even programmed, to go on. Operating on the personal level, Freud (1905) talks of a state of perpetual tension in intergenerational relations associated with sexuality.

Certainly there appears to be an endemic state of flux vis-à-vis authority on all levels, and in the 19th, 20th and 21st centuries we have witnessed a relentless turbulence. The challenge to the material and social dominance of particular classes and to the cultural dominance of an elitist establishment has come from different associations and influences during this period. Organised labour in the context of industrial employment and its facilitation of group assertion, mass warfare facilitating the generation of mass demands, mass education and the growth in global communication breaking down the controls of ignorance, isolation and the mystification of high culture – all of these changes have facilitated the assertion of the individual searching for fair shares in terms of material and intellectual goods and identity. Empathetic concern for the plight of the disadvantaged has undoubtedly also had some impact evidenced in the movements to abolish slavery, to improve working and environmental conditions and to tackle poverty. The moral institutions, including the churches, have been engaged with these endeavours, but, as noted, there have been other allegiances and impulses at work within established morality bolstering the very authorities and repressive relationships that these 'endeavours' seek to modify.

'Hell is other people' (Sartre, 1944): the changing designation of the 'other'

A third example of the jostling of impulses emerges in relation to the vexed question of the 'other'. In morality we see both the determined creation and adherence to boundaries between them and us, on the one hand, and the celebration of instances where barriers have been broken down and inclusiveness has prevailed, on the other. The emotions at play in the former include, alongside the setting of behaviour requirements and establishing conformity, feelings of group supremacy, fear of the different, the sense of solidarity in collective hate and the channelling of negative emotions onto a scapegoat. The latter is fuelled by matters of habit change, material benefits, shifts in the focus of ostracism and, for one reason or another, growing familiarity with the 'other', alongside the empathetic impulses favouring inclusion.

Religious institutions across faith groups have repeatedly demonstrated antipathy to the 'other'; the expression of their condemnation has ranged from social slights to wars and torture. And yet while there are antipathies, there are also episodes of coming together with multi faith activities and ceremonies demonstrating united fronts in relation to, for example, national crises or a particular moral stance. There is a United Nations sponsored Interfaith Harmony Week with participation across faiths. Periods of peaceful coexistence between religions may last for years until some shift in relations causes hostilities to erupt.

Within secularism, too, we have witnessed shifts in the domination of the left–right divide; communism versus capitalism has involved demonisation for many years, but as communism has dwindled the playing field has changed. The resurgence of nationalisms in the face of globalism is a further demonstration that the 'other' is always with us – but in different guises.

Morality in the human image – restless, changing, divided

These examples have drawn out the movement of behaviour and moralities over time. They have demonstrated the switches in priorities to and from particular impulses. Egotism, identity, security, hostility as well as caring have all staked their claim in different measure at different times. We have seen, too, the tensions and contradictions in the human psyche mirrored in morality's tussling. There are tensions and contradictions within the individual confronting antagonistic and complementary impulses and within groups operating both at one and at odds towards themselves and the 'other'.

The characteristics of morality revealed by cultural difference

Alongside the enhanced perspective gained from examining shifts in moral precepts over time, insights also emerge from an appreciation of the differences in morality between cultures. Here we flag up four areas of social relations exemplifying difference – the treatment of women; the control of behaviour; caring; and the relationship between the individual and wider community. There are many more.

Culture and women

The determination of the role of women is a prime example of the capacity of a culture to have a major and decidedly negative impact. Overtly patriarchal societies and linked religious doctrines have been associated with the restriction of female freedom and oppressive divorce and sex laws to the detriment of women's wellbeing. Violence against women is endemic, but varies widely between cultures with particularly high levels being prevalent in some societies (Fontes and McCloskey, 2011). While organisations such as the United Nations Committee monitoring the implementation of the Convention to Eliminate all Forms of Discrimination Against Women has highlighted discrimination against women in the UK (Owen, 2014) – and indeed the necessity for sexual equality legislation itself indicates the latent existence of such discrimination – the thrust of official expectation within the UK's secular state favours equality. However, different UK cultural traditions sustain a higher level of official discrimination, such as that exhibited by the exclusion of women from parts of the governing hierarchies of some religious institutions.

Culture and controlling behaviour

Possibly one of the most telling indications of the role of the empathetic impulses within a society's morality lies in its response to the transgression of norms. Punishment has elements of rehabilitation, retribution and deterrence. Societies vary considerably in the degree of retribution they deploy, tipping in some cases into vengeance and sadism. Thus, for example, we can see retribution ranging from high levels of harsh incarceration and capital punishment in the US to milder responses in most Western European countries (Liptak, 2008).

The upbringing of children presents significant cultural differences, particularly in relation to the management of children's behaviour. The veering of different societies and cultural groups between what has been described as authoritative parenting, providing a child with affection and moderate boundary setting, on the one hand, and authoritarian parenting, involving the strict exertion of discipline and liberal use of punishment, on the other, demonstrates very different cultural responses to that parent child caring instinct described by Darwin (Baumrind, 1967; Commission on Families and the Wellbeing of Children, 2005). Divergent attitudes to physical punishment have excised commentators and policy makers engaged with children's welfare. The potential for physical chastisement to degenerate into abuse is well documented (Commission on Families and the Wellbeing of Children, 2005). What is acceptable habitual assault of a child in one cultural tradition may be reprehensible child abuse in another.

Culture and caring

Differing concepts of family caring responsibilities has drawn extensive academic and policy interest. Prompted by tensions between the role of the state and the family, an academic paradigm has been developed by Esping-Andersen (1990; 1999) and applied to much subsequent research gauging the degree to which societies' caring provision for children, the elderly and other dependents is familial or de-familial. Marked differences emerge based on culture and material matters. Thus for example in affluent Germany expectations of high levels of family hands-on responsibilities for the caring of children and an emphasis on the maternal child bond has resulted in a large proportion of mothers declining paid work in favour of caring for their children (*Economist*, 2008). Sweden provides the contrasting approach with the highest number, 71.8 per cent, of mothers in work in 2012, and substantial caring responsibilities borne by the state (European Union, 2014).

Family caring extends beyond children to other vulnerable family members in particular the elderly. The question of elder care besets 21st century society as the proportion of the population constituting the vulnerable elderly increases with advances in living conditions and medicine. In some countries there is simultaneously a growing social orientation around individual fulfilment and a reluctance to spend time caring. The disparities in family responses to shouldering responsibilities shows a remarkable degree of cultural variability with countries such as Spain exhibiting a preference for familial responses and others, such as Sweden and The Netherlands, reliant to a greater degree on state sponsored care. There is a growing homogenisation facilitated by European institutions and the exchange of knowledge about practices, but nevertheless differences remain (Sundström et al, 2008). The isolation and loneliness of the elderly in individualistic societies typified by small unit family lifestyles sits in contrast with rather more inclusive societies where living orientation is around the extended family and an expectation of direct family care and responsibility. The question of isolation and its amelioration is closely associated with the empathetic emotions. The differing societal responses to that question demonstrate clearly how the habits of culture can and do overlay empathy allowing different impulses to hold sway. The role of culture is particularly stark when comparing communities within a country such as the UK with a population from differing cultural backgrounds brought together and operating with standard non-familial welfare facilities. Against this common context, the 2001 census found a greater degree of familial caring across generations amongst those from white British, Bangladeshi, Indian and Pakistani backgrounds compared with those from black African and Chinese backgrounds (Office of National Statistics, 2005).

Culture and the relationship between the individual and wider community

A theme and tension that runs through morality with a profound effect on social relations and public policy is the extent to which empathy is projected beyond the immediate family. Greene (2014) has written on differing individual psychological dispositions moderating the degree to which a person's sense of fairness and concern extends to a community, nation or even beyond. Notwithstanding individual psychology, culture with its impact in differentiating societies and groups within those societies is highly pertinent. Thus, for example, the predisposition of American society to focus on the welfare of immediate family and community contrasts with the tendency of some European welfare states to extend care more readily to a national and even international level. Work environments, too, can have an impact on the reach of concern with operations conducted in dangerous conditions such as mining drawing communities together for mutual support in contrast to jobs conducted in relative isolation within a competitive business environment.

Variety in the accommodation of impulses

This discussion has flagged up the impact of cultural diversity on the integration of impulses into human behaviour. The exhibition, prioritisation and accommodation of those impulses occur in response to varying pressures emerging from a plethora of cultures. Consequently, while scientific observation and research has undoubtedly demonstrated a commonality associated with the make-up of the brain and the existence of identifiable impulses, difference in the manifestation of those impulses also pertains.

The underlying role of impulses

Notwithstanding an acknowledgement of the substantial role of culture in the determination of behaviour, the scientific observation of the operation and derivation of impulses is critical. Impulses are at the root of culture and consequent behaviour and require as full an understanding as possible. While other influences are at work, it is the interrelationship of culture with impulses that is the trigger for behaviour both in its delivery and moral conceptualisation. The complexity of that relationship is daunting and, while the study of behaviour has been the subject of extensive research across disciplines embracing psychology, anthropology, economic behaviour and sociology, its full comprehension continues to prove elusive.

Human group behaviour remains to a disconcertingly large extent unpredictable. Chaos theory to the effect that the smallest of incidents can have an extraordinary thread of interconnectedness, an effect that cannot be anticipated, appears to fit at least metaphorically (Kellert,

1993; Werndl, 2009). Uncertainty there is, but, while predictability may be out of our grasp, there are connections to be made and it is important to be alerted to these in managing morality. Some synchronisation is needed between impulses and culture and an understanding that when they are substantially out of kilter, tensions and possibly social disruption may be anticipated.

The suppression of sexuality as described by D.H. Lawrence (1913; 1920; 1928) in his condemnation of a stultifying morality provides a graphic example of such dislocation and its implications. Victorian and Edwardian society operated a taboo on the expression of sexual feelings. Matrimony and children conceived within marriage were the public expression of things sexual. It was an aspect of the culture of the day that was embodied in the morality professed by established institutions and the law, with divorce very difficult to achieve and associated with shame. Alongside a culture of desexualised family life sustained by the moral institutions of the church and the law was a manifestation of sexuality in an underworld where gender power relations saw sex bought and sold. It was a hypocrisy that became documented in pictorial art with, for example, Manet's naked women picnicking with clothed gentlemen in the park in *Le dejeuner sur l'herbe* (1863); a shocking exposé for a culture so far suspended from its impulses. Its undoing began with this exposure, but needed verbal analysis. Culture started to shift to a more open acknowledgement of sexual needs. Post World War I, with a dislocation of the status quo and progress on the emancipation front, there was an era of sexual licence within circles of the dominant classes. It was a licence that was to be affirmed and augmented in the Second World War in a process that was rather less associated with frivolity and more to do with the liberation associated with separation and mortality. There was a movement to discuss sexuality openly in the literature of the avant garde that both mirrored and propelled change, bringing understanding and expectations of behaviour closer to a hitherto unacknowledged impulse. Lawrence provided the obvious marker with his frank, for those times, description of sex, its frustration and fulfilment. Away from literature was the investigation of the psyche; Freud (1905) put sexuality and its dominion over relationships from the early days infancy into the public arena. There was a greater acknowledgement of the uncontrollable and pervasive nature of the sexual impulse. However, while culture changed, institutional morality and the law took decades to follow suit; the dislocation continued with repeated frictions permeating the conduct and literature of sexual behaviour. It would be an error to anticipate the easy achievement of synchronisation across impulses, culture and moral regulation, but the history of sexuality in the 19th and 20th centuries certainly tells a tale of the toll of frustration and unhappiness where the dislocation is unbearably acute.

What is left for commonality?

The proposition that morality is not about a single direction prevalence of empathy over the spectrum of human impulses, but rather that prioritisation is multidirectional and in a state of constant flux poses some problems for discourses favouring a cut and dry analysis and solution. The lack of predictability in human behaviour as a consequence of a fluid jostling of impulses and external influences poses questions for the project of shaping behavioural responses in a particular direction and certainly undermines any simplistic conviction associated with the concept of progress.

With this analysis how much are we left with of commonality across moralities? Rather more than might be thought. While empathy may not be the single point of reference for the ordering of actions, what is apparent is that morality is about addressing the multiplicity of human impulses. This does not necessarily entail prioritisation, although it may do so. Rather it is about an accommodation whereby impulses are managed within a framework for living.

Relativism

Bearing this scenario in mind, is relativism still at odds with commonality? The concepts are prima facie contradictory. Certainly total relativism, whereby there is no common thread to morality, runs counter to the proposition that human impulses are at the core of morality. However, as discussed, variation within this impulse framework is prevalent with its derivation traceable to divergence in culture, individual human characteristics and external influences. Boundaries may become apparent when impulses are excessively denied, but there is, as evidenced by the range of viable societies, considerable scope for variation in human relations and behaviours.

Commonality associated with a host of impulses is a more inclusive phenomenon than commonality linked to the prioritisation and superior status of a particular impulse such as empathy. Relativism would have a highly circumscribed field of operation in the context of Darwin's empathetic morality. The options are greater when the scope of impulses included in the conceptualisation of morality is expansive. In the analysis of morality in this discussion, which falls within the 'expansive' rather than the 'circumscribed' category, commonality and relativism have the possibility to coexist.

Threading through this description of the way in which the management of impulses is acted out in human relations, one is struck by the degree of differentiation and change in the moral landscape. That fluidity has posed difficulties for moral philosophers as discussed in Chapter Two – difficulties not associated with whether variation is true when reflecting on human behaviour and the reality of cultural impact, but difficulties in terms of what we *should* be seeking from morality. Mary Midgley (1984), amongst others, has expressed anxiety over a vapid, anything goes, liberalism. Midgley's position here is one of aspiration. It is important to distinguish between how things are and how individuals and societies might wish them to be; because of their interrelationship, the line between these two concepts is all too often blurred.

For some societies a relativistic aspirational stance may not be preferred. However, for a largely secular society such as that which pertains in the UK, a relativistic position may be feasible. A protective bottom line of human rights is a widely accepted point of reference that might be adopted in a society that acknowledges the fluidity and relativity of morality and is at ease with a liberal response thereto; the possible role of human rights in such a context is discussed in Chapter Five.

Revelatory systems of morality versus secular moral philosophy

Within the multiple moral structures on offer we have revelatory systems involving the metaphysical and systems of secular moral philosophy argued within the confines of human relations. The division between the two, as described in Chapter One, has been acrimonious, with the essence of self-perception and world views at stake. There are divisions, but also synchronisations that necessitate teasing out and recognition for the purpose of managing morality in a multicultural society.

Moral revelation

Tensions

Revelatory systems, with their orientation around metaphysical edicts, present difficulties in respect of the need for adjustment from time to time when impulses, culture and moral institutions are subject to excessive tension. Commonly recognised failures have been noted in Christianity in respect of gender and power relations. The Church of England and the Catholic Church have conspicuously held back the position of women having actively hampered moves away from a patriarchal society towards one with some gender equality aspirations. From the inclusion for many years past its sell by date of the wifely obedience matrimonial vow through to the risible spectacle of the haggle over women becoming clergy and bishops, the record has been one of stultifying oppressive social conservatism. In respect of sexual relations there has also been reluctance to move with advances facilitating a more liberal approach to sexual activity. There has been the stalling of the use of birth control in some quarters; similarly the liberalisation of the abortion law has had its strongest opposition in the faith lobby.

> Therefore We base Our words on the first principles of a human and Christian doctrine of marriage when We are obliged once more to declare that the direct interruption of the generative process already begun and, above all, all direct abortion, even for therapeutic reasons, are to be absolutely excluded as lawful means of regulating the number of children. Equally to be condemned, as the magisterium of the Church has affirmed on many occasions, is direct sterilisation, whether of the man or of the woman, whether permanent or temporary. Similarly excluded is any action which either before, at the moment of, or after sexual intercourse, is specifically intended to prevent procreation— whether as an end or as a means. (Pope Paul VI, 1968)

The movement towards liberalising attitudes and lifting the prohibition of same sex relations has had its staunchest opponents in the revelatory moralities; there have been repeated instances of clashes with equalities legislation over discriminatory treatment of gay couples and there has been sustained opposition to the introduction of gay marriage (BBC 2009; Ross and Bingham, 2012).

Moving away from matters sexual, there are examples in medicine where advances that have been made have met intransigence in some religious responses. Recently we have seen faith based opposition to a tested and government approved medical intervention involving three parents input into the genetic make-up of a child; under this procedure faulty mitochondrial DNA in a mother's egg would be replaced with healthy DNA from a second woman thereby removing the risk of a range of diseases developing in the child. Religious opposition has been voiced on ethical grounds with concerns that parenthood would be diluted (Sample, 2015).

There are more shocking examples. In his book, *The Children Act*, Ian McEwan cites the issue of blood transfusion, a medical practice shunned by Jehovah's Witnesses because of the following words in Genesis 9.4: 'Only flesh with its life, its blood, you must not eat'. The novel draws on a real life legal case involving an attempted blocking of blood transfusion to save the life of a boy by his parents adhering to the Jehovah Witness faith. There was a legal overruling of the parents' position, but when the child reached the age of legal majority he was able to make a medical decision in respect of his treatment and chose to adhere to the faith in which he had been brought up. The medical advice was rejected and death ensued (McEwan, 2014). In this case a religion locked in a moral stance associated with out-of-date health precepts seriously contravened the impulse of self-preservation.

Moderation and revelation

While there are extreme cases like this, there are also instances where revelatory morality has been modified to move with shifting cultural norms. Some churches/faiths have moved ground to accommodate divorce, contraception and homosexuality. The days of severe retribution for gainsaying doctrinal edicts have long passed in the European Christian churches. It is also pertinent that revelatory systems with their hosting of the spectrum of impulses in art, music and narrative have been instrumental in creating, sustaining and reflecting societies and cultures in the round. Their multifaceted nature is able to address the constituents of living in a comprehensive and subtle as well as a particular and overt fashion.

Critically in reviewing the traits of revelatory systems it is important to reflect on the major variation within those systems, particularly in relation to the use of rational argument and the evidence that some engage with religion principally as a mythological illustration and point of connection for the human enterprise (Cupitt, 1984). The principal religions of the 21st century have substantial components of rational debate within their discourse.

Taking Islam by way of example, Malik (2014) has identified a traditional and rational philosophical divide in the early stages of the religion's development. The traditionalists such as Al-Ghazali conceived the revelations of an omnipotent god as the only reference to truth. The rationalists, such as Ibn Sina, on the other hand, placed greater emphasis on the capacity of humans using their own endeavours to reach conclusions that coincide with those of a rational god. Ibn Sina used a process of rationalisation to argue the case for the existence of god and the value of Islamic ethical practices (Malik, 2014). The rationalist school in Islam became overshadowed by two schools of belief. One supported a detailed literal interpretation of revelation; the other had strong elements of mysticism. Al-Ghazali (2002) engaged in a critique of rationalism and with *The Incoherence of Philosophers* established the supremacy of a defined belief system, transgression of which merited death. The argument has been made that the ascendancy of the traditionalists was motored by a defensive response to the challenge posed by rationalist thinking on free will to both the state's power and religious orthodoxy. Alongside the clear cut and strictly enforced set of revelatory rules and laws associated with traditionalists – the Sunni orthodoxy – there developed a strain of Islamic belief sustained within the Shia doctrine that was more associated with the soul – a mystical coming closer to god, placing greater emphasis on human responsibility and free will. Within the latter strand we see some of the rationalist's legacy (Malik, 2014).

In the Christian tradition too we can see the proposition of human rationalism forming a highly significant component in theological thinking. In the 13th century St Thomas Aquinas (1975; 2007) was a prominent advocate of rationalism; his extensive discourse has dominated Christian enquiry from the Middle Ages to the present. For him achieving human beings potential to engage with reason was the essential purpose and function of lives. He had a clear affinity with Aristotle's virtue ethics viewing fulfilment as the essential goal, but defining that fulfilment as being at one with god. Aquinas, like Aristotle, considered that the conditions for human flourishing needed to enable them to achieve their rational and virtuous potential were of major import. Physical capacity and moral responsibility were jointly pertinent to human fulfilment. In 20th-century Christianity, Don Cupitt, most prominently in his television series *The Sea of Faith* (1984), has been an advocate of the interpretation of metaphysical revelation as metaphorical, as illustrative and offering myth. He follows Christian spiritual practice and ethical standards without belief in the metaphysics of Christianity. Cupitt describes this approach as non-realist Christian 'solar living'.

As one examines these strands of moderate religious thinking involving engagement in rational argument and the promotion of a concept of humanity as a rational animal capable of making choices and generating change, it is evident that there is potential for measured debate around morality. There is within the rational revelatory approach the potential to respond and adapt to change, reflecting attitudes and behaviours as they currently are in a materially and conceptually shifting world. Conversely it must be recognised that traditionalist revelatory cultural patterns present a continuing challenge, if not an impediment, to this process.

> One of the great selling powers of monotheistic religions throughout their history has been their importance as a bedrock of moral values. Without religious faith, runs the argument, we cannot anchor our moral truths or truly know right from wrong. Without belief in God we will be lost in a miasma of moral nihilism. Yet the transformation in the first four centuries not just in the fortunes of Christianity but also in the ethical ideas that animated it reveals the flexibility of religious precepts. Believers may see religious ethics as absolute. They have to, in order to believe. But God himself appears to be highly pragmatic. The absoluteness of religious precepts can seem unforgiving, less so the precepts themselves. The success of religious morality derives from its ability to cut its beliefs according to social needs while at the same time insisting that such beliefs are sacred because they are God-given. (Malik, 2014, pp 75–6)

Malik's commentary rings with a deal of truth in relation to the degree to which traditionalist revelatory morality meets the apparent social structure needs of the population at the point of early evolution of the host religion. The point of omission from the quote, however, is that enforcement of moral precepts through the word of god is of such a durable nature that it is hard to change; metaphysical super glue exerts a heavy price for its durability.

The humanist philosopher Grayling puts the tendency of religions towards stasis rather more strongly, some might say bitterly.

> The open-mindedness of science, and its need to thrive in the fresh air of challenge and debate, contrasts sharply with religion. Religions are governed by inflexibilities of dogma and tradition, in defence of which – incredibly – many people are prepared to kill.
>
> … Among the vast differences between science and religion is the fact that the former is progressive and cumulative, the latter static and backward-looking. Perhaps

mankind's hope lies in this fact, for it suggests that open-minded curiosity might eventually defeat the superstitions that still oppress many. Voltaire once remarked that he loved the man who seeks truth, but hated the man who claims to have found it. There are no prizes for guessing which was the scientist, which the priest. (Grayling, 2004, pp 220–1)

Secular systems

Revelatory systems have an historical and current cultural presence that permeates thinking, and it may be anticipated that they will continue to have a prominent role in the national determination of moral issues in the UK. However, the supposition that they should have a lead function has been vociferously challenged in recent years. As we have noted in Chapter One, there are concerns over the disproportionate power of the religious establishment in the UK which secular organisations such as the British Humanist Association are trying to contain. As well as a disputation over the legitimacy of belief, there are deep concerns over the socially conservative tendencies and hostility to progressive change within revelatory systems. However, highly pertinent to the management of morality is the evidence that this resistance to accommodation is not the provenance of the revelatory camp alone. There are some secular moralities that are not open to an inclusive, measured debate and which have features in common with the very aspects of revelatory morality that are the subject of criticism by secularists.

There has been a tendency in some strands of secular thinking to focus on a single issue or particular influence affecting behaviour. Thus as we have seen the role of sex has dominated psychoanalytical discourses, while power relations have been viewed by others as central to human motivation. In aspirational philosophies we have seen esoteric philosophical positions argued to the extremes, divorcing the model from the reality of human impulse and behaviour – Kant's placing of the notion of immutable 'duty' on a pedestal being a prime example. Concepts such as the 'veil of ignorance' proposed by Rawls for the establishment of a moral code are similarly distanced from the reality of the source of human thought. Breadth of understanding often eludes the process of single-minded cogitative engagement. Houses of cards are a constant danger when thinking is not grounded in the acknowledgement of the operation of conflicting behavioural realities.

Flexibility within a broad vision capable of moderation is perhaps most starkly missing in the atheistic field from what has come to be known as the secular religion of communism. Communism sought through rational argument to establish something of a heaven on earth; by following the logic of changes in the ownership of the means of production, it anticipated the achievement of a more egalitarian society. Communism derived its hold on large parts of the globe from a treatise reviewing socioeconomic relations with an in depth original analysis that holds good albeit that an empire has come and gone in its name. The thesis made an important contribution to the understanding of social dynamics, but the interpretation was one track; it understated the function of culture. And its implementation as a political model was single minded and blinkered.

Tribalism

As the world split into two secular giants, communism and capitalism, a world stage drama ensued stretching out over much of the 20th century. What transpired was the emergence of more than two divergent interpretations of social evolution, although that was significant enough; it was 'tribalism' – a human impulse that is one of the strongest motivations of collective behaviour across religious and secular systems.

Tribalism is a unifier of those within the tribe and an excluder of those outside. It is associated with hostility to the cultural 'other'. Tribalism has been part and parcel of the revelatory religious offer, but as a human trait it goes beyond metaphysical beliefs. It is one of the most dominant human motivations offering identity and safety. Reflecting on group behaviour at different levels suggests that it is one of the most powerful human needs. It appears in the separation of classes, political groups, regions of all sizes, nations, ethnic groups, religions, institutions and even sports teams.

Since the decline and fall of the communist secular empire, nationalisms have proliferated filling the tribal vacuum. There was little of religion associated with the nationalisms arising from this insurgence; the struggle for freedom from communism was not primarily a religious one, although religion sometimes featured in disputes. The dominance of the American capitalist formula in the wake of the communist demise has, however, pushed tribal opposition into the religious sphere – commonly perceived in Islamic states and groupings, but also present in other religions. A Russian nationalist resurgence with aspirations to empire is also in the frame in respect of the old communist East European buffer states. In the 20th and 21st centuries we have seen tribalism in secular versus secular disputes and in secular versus religious ones.

This tale of identities and levels of commitment and antipathy is illustrative of the importance of tribalism across the revelatory and rational divide. Together with its ubiquitous nature, the tenaciousness and deep-rooted emotional nature of tribalism's hold presents the management of morality with one of its greatest challenges.

Overview

The complexity of motives influencing human behaviour, their tensions and contradictions, is considerable. They go beyond the dichotomy between sociability and competition. They cross a range of short- and long-term impulses, some innate, some cultural and some of which, despite the advances of behavioural science, we do not yet understand. As well as a strong empathetic strand, they comprise urges within the human drama associated with power, sex, self-preservation and the assertion of the ego and identity. And at least as influential with considerable staying power is a tendency to comply with habit and group norms. The description in this chapter has demonstrated the volatility of the processes at work vying between stability and eruption. The contention is that morality is a significant player in this maelstrom, not as a simple promoter of the social instincts, but rather as a manager of the human condition. While morality is a vehicle for the reconciliation of conflicting impulses, it is about the management of these in all their complexity without the presumption of a dominant single motivation. The emerging proposition that morality is concerned with the accommodation of impulses within varied and changing cultural contexts combines a degree of commonality and relativism that would benefit from recognition and synchronisation in the public policy arena. In effecting such a process the constantly mutating alignments and antagonisms of revelatory, secular and tribal influences will require a fully informed and sophisticated understanding. There will be a need to unearth and work with the potential flexibility that exists across both revelatory and secular traditions – and to minimise the intransigence and emotionalism of tribal affiliations.

FOUR

The challenges and benefits of a new role for public policy

The consideration of the nature of morality in Chapter Three has demonstrated its breadth and varied manifestations. Common properties and points of divergence have been identified – a critical exercise for the purpose of developing public policy. Recognition has been given to the respective roles of analysis and aspiration in respect of human behaviour within moral discourse, their differing but overlapping nature. Through an assessment of both these aspects of moral debate a proposition of commonality has been formulated across the elastic and contentious phenomena of moralities. The finding that morality is about the accommodation of the jostling of divergent impulses scientifically located within the brain is the point of reference for this commonality. The implementation of the accommodation in different ways in response to cultural and material pressures offers a synergy with relativism.

In addition, the discussion has unpicked the tensions between two of the principal players in the morality stakes – systems grounded in revelation on the one hand and, on the other, those that focus on rational argument frequently honed from a particular stance on the human condition. These differences are the subject of heated debate in the context of affairs ranging from interpersonal relations and responses to scientific advances to internecine power struggles on the world stage and pervasive tribalism. There are nevertheless some sympathetic fusions and similarities across the divide, which provide points of connection. An understanding of both the tensions and common threads that coexist across the metaphysical and non-revelatory split is essential in order to assess possible ways of enhancing public policy responses to moral questions.

The conclusions of this probe point to the existence of a genuinely identifiable phenomenon of morality with biological roots verified by scientific investigation and of sufficient moment and validity to command recognition in the public policy arena. It is also a shifting and variable entity and as a consequence requires monitoring and gauging in order to deliver a timely, appropriate and effective public policy response. It is a sphere with severe tensions that requires a focused, inclusive public policy and an ongoing examination of the breadth of the evidence. In combination the findings across commonality and relativism, the tensions and antagonisms, indicate the necessity for a significant element of management in the public domain and the establishment of formal consideration and debate of the morality–public policy interface supported by an analytical resource.

Undertaking such an enterprise is a daunting task, in particular in the context of an open recognition of the function of morality as being about the accommodation of a wide spectrum of impulses. In this chapter we consider the challenges and benefits associated with this direction of thought and development. The challenges flagged up relate to the discomfort of the different take on the nature of humankind, an undermining of the 'progressive' aspiration in public policy and the amorphous nature of relativism. The benefits encompass greater transparency and an enhanced capacity to address the reality of human behaviour and changes in morality.

Challenges

The tenacity of the concept of progress

> But the myth of progress is extremely potent. When it loses its power those who have lived by it are – as Conrad put it, describing Kayerts and Carlier – 'like those lifelong prisoners who, liberated after many years, do not know what use to make of their freedoms'. When faith in the future is taken from them, so is the image they have of themselves. If they then opt for death, it is because without that faith they can no longer make sense of living. (Gray, 2013, p 7)

The language used in public policy tends to be one of aspiring to perfection rather than more neutrally – and realistically – managing tensions in the context of the coexistence of multiple impulses and cultural relativism. The proposition championed by Darwin and others that empathy and the social instincts are prioritised in morality has an association with expectations of progress and questioning this presumption will pose something of a challenge.

The contention frequently made in moral discourse is that the enlightenment and its endorsement of progressive liberalism and a belief in humanity's capacity to achieve social transformation are behind us. The conviction that social division would fall in the wake of progress began to wane in the 19th century. Fear of intellectual anarchy and social disintegration were instrumental in its demise. Coupled with a dwindling belief in god across tranches of society in Western Europe, this has given rise to the philosophy of retreat and limited expectation. The experience of human depravity on a massive scale in the Second World War and the failure of the major endeavours at social transformation, specifically communism with its associated oppression, are perceived as having placed the final nail in coffin of enlightened expectations.

> The death of God only made sense against the background of a new kind of faith: faith in humans being capable of acting rationally and morally without guidance from beyond. It was that faith that drove the Enlightenment humanism and the optimism of the eighteenth and nineteenth centuries. By the end of the nineteenth century that faith, too, had begun to be eaten away. The history of the twentieth century – two world wars, the Depression and the Holocaust, Auschwitz and the gulags, climate change and ethnic cleansing – helped further gnaw away at Enlightenment hope. We no longer believe, as Canadian scholar and politician Michael Ignatieff has observed, that 'material progress entails or enables moral progress'. (Malik, 2014, p 341–2)

And yet the evidence points to a residual adherence to a way of thinking and operation that endorses the progressive. Malik himself describes the principal split in contemporary moral philosophy as being between relativism and a universalism with similarities to enlightenment convictions.

The continued hold of progressive conviction can be seen in the negative, even vitriolic, response to John Gray's contention that it is a misconception to think that the human emotional disposition, or 'hard wiring', can be changed or 'progressed'. He notes that to date this disposition has only been subject to tinkering in the psychological sphere. This stasis stands in stark contrast to the staggering impact achieved in material matters – scientific investigation and the effecting of change on the environment in which we live.

> Science and technology are cumulative, whereas ethics and politics deal with recurring dilemmas. Whatever they are called, torture and slavery are universal evils; but these evils cannot be consigned to the past like redundant theories

in science. They return under different names; torture as enhanced interrogation techniques, slavery as human trafficking. (Gray, 2013, p 75)

Gray's argument that we are as we are may have lacked an attempt to determine how public policy should relate to such a proposition – but the nature of the dismissal of the book emitted an emotion beyond merely decrying this omission (Conrad, 2013; McCarthy, 2014). That it touched a raw nerve is the inevitable conclusion to be drawn.

Responses to another major commentary on the human condition, Steven Pinker's *The Better Angels of our Nature. A History of Violence and Humanity* (2012), are drawn in a similar pro-progress vein. Pinker offers a major documentation of human behavioural development. His conclusion is that the sum of violent behaviour globally and over time has dwindled as more people experienced a tamed environment; a collectivised mode of living has taken hold and consequently more peaceable ways of dispute resolution have been engaged with. Commentaries have interpreted the findings as a full blown endorsement of the innate nature of human progress, making scant reference to Pinker's clear position that humans have not changed and that a capacity for violence is as prevalent today as ever it was notwithstanding changes in the habits of social relations.

> Human nature, as evolution left it, is not up to the challenge of getting us into the blessedly peaceful cell in the upper left corner of the matrix. Motives like greed, fear, dominance, and lust keep drawing us towards aggression. And though a major work-around, the threat of tit-for-tat vengeance, has the potential to bring about cooperation if the game is repeated, in practice it is miscalibrated by self-serving biases and often results in cycles of feuding rather than stable deterrence. (Pinker, 2012, p 840)

Amelioration

There is, too, an offshoot of progressive thinking – 'amelioration' – that seeks to address the contra-indicators undermining the enlightenment model of thought. The possibility of ameliorating institutions and social relations has been put forward as a second best option in the face of the evidence of human failing and depravity. The thesis is that some improvement can be made, that by working through a cultural dimension changes can be effected and that these will impact incrementally offering scope for ameliorative development. The colloquialism might be 'two steps forward, one step back'. The dizzying heights of aspiration associated with the enlightenment are to be abjured in favour of a more modest hope, but which, nevertheless, has something of the same belief or mode of thought – the emotional gear of progression.

It may be queried where the difference lies between a philosophy of amelioration and one of accommodation. It is one of orientation. An accommodating stance is one that does not anticipate advance to a destination on a trajectory of progressive change. Rather it is accepting of a variety of impulses with expectation of fluctuation in the way such impulses interact. It is less concerned to channel that fluctuation in a particular direction, but is rather more geared to providing an enabling facility with a rights shield for the protection of vulnerability. The contention is that accommodation will provide a more satisfactory living arrangement because it is closer to the reality of the way human intercourse operates than a misdirected pathway that entails delusion and disappointment.

Administration and the habit of 'progress speak'

> Together we can even make politics and politicians work better. And if we can do that, we can do anything. Yes, together we can do anything. (Conservative Party manifesto, 2010, p iii)
>
> **Britain will be better with new Labour**
>
> 'Our case is simple: that Britain can and must be better.'
>
> 'The vision is one of national renewal, a country with drive, purpose and energy.' (Labour Party manifesto, 1997, p 1)

The habituation of the concept of progress is perhaps most particularly in evidence in the speeches of politicians – party manifestos and other public policy aspirational documents. Phrases such as 'ensure it never happens again' are the common parlance in responding to criminal activity, under par performance and failure in public institutions. It is blithely trotted out following tragedies and disappointments of one sort or another flying in the face of an apparently unstoppable recidivism.

> All human institutions – families and churches, police forces and anarchists – are stained by crime. Explaining human nastiness by reference to corrupt institutions leaves a question: why are human's so attached to corruption?

Clearly the answer is in the human animal itself. (Gray, 2013, p 10)

There are some prominent topical issues falling into this pattern of fallacious redemption – astounded outrage followed by the vow of never again and thereafter the inevitable recurrence, a recurrence that could have been anticipated had society not been in collective denial. According to the Managing Director of the International Monetary Fund, Christine Lagarde, speaking to the Conference on Inclusive Capitalism, the financial world has taken no more than four years to resume many of its follies and business as usual following the bank driven financial crash of 2008.

> ... the behavior of the financial sector has not changed fundamentally in a number of dimensions since the crisis. While some changes in behavior are taking place, these are not deep or broad enough. The industry still prizes short-term profit over long-term prudence, today's bonus over tomorrow's relationship.
>
> Some prominent firms have even been mired in scandals that violate the most basic ethical norms—LIBOR and foreign exchange rigging, money laundering, illegal foreclosure.
>
> To restore trust, we need a shift toward greater integrity and accountability. We need a stronger and systematic ethical dimension. (Lagarde, 2014)

The failings of care for the vulnerable, ranging from neglect to sadistic practices, continues to astonish, and, while checks are instituted from time to time, matters repeatedly fall beneath the scrutiny radar with the self-evident human trait of victimisation at some level of commission or omission receiving inadequate attention. Inquiries into lapses in care, such as those conducted in respect of the Orchid View and Winterbourne homes, are frequently in the news and in 2014 the BBCs Panorama programme revealed systemic neglect and abuse across a number of care institutions. The Equality and Human Rights Commission (2011) has similarly found sub-standard care provided for the elderly in their own homes.

Paedophilia and child abuse – this is not a 20th- and 21st- century disease of the psyche as news bulletins, scaled up police operations and the accounts of establishment connivance and social service lapse all imply. It is an endemic human condition behind wraps, a denial born of a complexity of hypocrisy and disbelief that prompts incantation of shock. With child abuse common from top to bottom of society, the dismay expressed is hard to buy, and yet with the strong hold that progression exerts over collective thinking, it is real enough. It is described rather graphically in this article in the *Telegraph*:

> Outrage at Jimmy Savile conceals the fact that our culture encourages paedophilia.
>
> Yet another bloody article about Jimmy Savile. We read more and more about the horrors that went on and the now incontestable fact that others knew it was happening, and we get all shouty and indignant. It reveals the irksome, irritating side of Twitter, the tabloid press, self-published blogs and the loud, chatty guy in the pub. The moral high ground. The furious bleating and self-righteousness of the whiter-than-white populace.
>
> The outcry will not do any good at all. How many times since "Never again" has it happened again?
>
> … Newspapers happily show pictures of 14-year-old girls sunbathing and use sexual language to describe them while at the same time appearing indignant and appalled at the crimes of Savile, Glitter et al.
>
> The culture of celebrity has the same shroud of secrecy, power and authority as the Church. Why on earth should we be surprised at sexual abuse going on in those circles? The only thing that surprises me is that people actually seem surprised. In any environment where there is power, there will be an abuse of that power. (Rhodes, 2012)

The danger of denying habitual behaviour trends in the human condition is perceptively and eloquently described by Richard Holloway, the former Bishop of Edinburgh.

> We create these heartbreaks for ourselves time after time in life, but we make them worse by our failure to recognise that they are the rule not the exception. All our paradises are lost paradises. The way we let unrealistic expectations destroy flawed yet retrievable relationships is sad enough; a bigger hazard of our Edenic fantasies is when we transpose them onto the collective level, whether in religion or politics. More misery and disillusionment has been visited on humanity by its search for the perfect society and the

perfect faith than by any other cause. The fantasy of crafting the ideal society or establishing the perfect religious system is far from being an endearing form of romanticism: it all too easily turns into terror. Listening to the voice that commands us to follow its perfect blueprint for rebuilding Eden usually results not in heaven but in hell on earth, whether in the home-grown or a built-for-export version. (Holloway, 2009, p 136)

In making his plea for recognition of the human condition, Holloway is fully cognisant of the nature of human impulses as indicated in this extract:

It is no accident that critics and commentators frequently link sex and violence together as though they were a single phenomenon, *sexandviolence*. This is more than a recognition that they are both primal forces in nature, including human nature. It is to recognise that they are erotically charged, packed with the possibility of giving pleasure to participant and onlooker, described by Auden as 'the concupiscence of the oppressor'. …

The erotic possibilities of the theatre of public cruelty have been exploited by humanity for centuries, right down to the reality TV shows of today. We have been geniuses at crafting set pieces of torture and execution, designed to entertain as well as deter the public. Before they were banned, seats at public executions were as keenly sought after as tickets for violent blockbuster films are in our own day. (Holloway, 2009, pp 14–15)

The capacity to take on board a new perspective of accommodation in place of progress

The questioning of progressive assumptions does not imply an endorsement of a conservative repression consequent on a negative perception of the human condition. Rather the intent is to frame a model that has a realistic understanding of human impulse and interaction, to scope a public policy discourse in terms, not of repressing and controlling, but of managing and accommodating without an expectation of changing the unchangeable.

While the aim may not be negativity, the danger is that a more balanced orientation of the public policy platform may engender a feeling of despondency. Furthermore the open discussion of the breadth of impulses may cast something of a harsh light on the human condition and the mesh of culture and behaviours. This anxiety should, however, be viewed in the context of human resilience and ability to accept uncomfortable new perspectives.

There are many examples of where such novelty has been absorbed into the collective consciousness. Freud with his revelation of the nature of infant sexuality is an obvious example. The early onset of sexuality, its pervasive impact on behaviour and mental and physical wellbeing, and the elements of antagonism and aggression linked to sexual jealousy were findings that were somewhat in contrast to strains of public feeling that identified childhood with innocence and kept sexuality hidden (Freud, 1905). And yet much of the core of Freudian thought came to be accepted in common understanding; in the words of the poet Auden at the time of Freud's death in 1939 he had become 'a whole climate of opinion / under whom we conduct our different lives' (Auden, 1940). Darwin's thesis contained in *On the Origin of Species* (1859) had perhaps even greater potential to upset the applecart. With its substitution of natural selection for the religious narrative of the creation of man, this altered understanding of the human place in the universe brought with it the threat of undermining moral order. With morality ingrained through the churches and the whole entwined with both social hierarchy and national governance, the establishment was perceived as being under attack. As significantly, these automatic natural selection processes that have little to do with the elevated individual or the supernatural jeopardised people's sense of emotional security. Yet despite the dimension of the psychological reorientation required, there has been a full acceptance of Darwin's findings in mainstream thought.

Response to novelty of course operates at different levels. What may be accepted logically can be compartmentalised with residual ties to old understandings keeping hold of the emotions. The scale of the universe, the slippery notion of time, the certainty of the future dissolution of the earth – as well as the development of life and its mutation through natural selection and the workings of the human psyche – these truths we may know, but they are kept at a distance. There is much intellectual acceptance alongside a dose of emotional denial.

Living with such a duality and conflict is not atypical in the history of thought. The gargoyles around the tops of Christian churches are testament to a bygone era of pre-Christian beliefs. There is a coexistence evidenced in the merging of Christian celebrations around the life of Christ with pagan festivals geared to reflecting the passage of the seasons, in particular the winter solstice with the birth of Christ and the spring awakening with Christ's death and resurrection. This dual functioning, with past presumptions slipping into the realms of myth and backdrop, has worked surprisingly effectively with accommodations that have nevertheless seen new understandings prevail in the mainstream of social business. The sensation that the sun rises even though we know it does not – ditto that the earth is the centre of the universe even though we most decidedly know it is not – are all examples of the duality of perceptions that are the stuff of living and the limitations of a human centric orientation. Residual emotional conviction of the sublime human individual with autonomy, free will and a soul alongside the permanence of humanity with a destiny – are all part of this human centric orientation: so, too with engagement with the comfort of 'progress'.

The feeling that progress is the raison d'être of human endeavour has survived at a certain level of consciousness despite the proclaimed demise of the enlightenment in the wake of 19th- and 20th-century reality checks with human destructiveness, a falling short of achieving social transformation and an enhanced understanding of human psychological development.

While it may be anticipated that there will be a continuation of residual feelings of identity associated with the enlightenment, the question is whether that hold can be contained sufficiently to enable a different approach to flourish. There has perhaps not been a sufficient reorientation of thought and discourse in the public sphere offering an alternative model for social living – a loss without the flotation of alternatives. That is the conceptual offer being put forward here. It would constitute major change and discomfort, but also present some considerable benefits.

The challenge of relativism

A significant element of the proposition that morality is about the management of impulses is the acknowledgement of the capacity of humans to evince different cultural responses in the moral sphere. This relativistic interpretation of human behaviour gives rise to a possible, and arguably logical, next step, which would be for public policy to facilitate rather than constrict moral difference – in effect adopting relativism as an in principle aspiration. Such an approach has had its advocates within liberal ethics promoting tolerance (Mill, 1859) and amongst philosophers who recognise the existence of moral diversity as a fact of life (Strawson, 1974). Relativism has also had its critics despairing at the prospect of incoherence and a society at sea (Midgley, 1984). As with the undermining of a model of progression, this quandary described in Chapter Two does present a serious challenge. A possible circumvention of the difficulty posed to societal cohesion by relativism is to sustain diversity within agreed limits. A framework of fundamental rights for the purpose of protection – in particular protection of the vulnerable – might provide such a bottom line. Although they have of necessity a cultural heritage, rights formulated as 'human rights' do have global currency. As discussed in Chapter Five, adherence to their precepts would provide sufficient societal cohesion to enable a high degree of relativism to be sustained. And, it may be argued, that such an endorsement of relativism would be appropriate for UK society with its culturally diverse population.

Fighting shy of a morality and public policy analytical tool – a minor challenge

The existence of a morality and public policy analysis resource to support government would facilitate the adoption of considered, timely and flexible public policy responses to a fluid morality accommodating impulses in a community with a rich cultural mix. While the establishment of such a resource would itself present something of a challenge in the face of ingrained governmental recoil from matters moral, there is little doubt that such reservations could be overcome as they have been in the past with regard to sensitivities over the introduction of race and gender equality legislation and associated institutions. The creation of commissions to examine the ethics of scientific developments also provides a reassuring precedent of adaptable thinking. This governmental apparatus gives a clear indication that taking the plunge works wonders.

Benefits

Bertrand Russell makes a moving plea for facing the facts:

Fear is the principal reason why men are so unwilling to admit facts and so anxious to wrap themselves round in a warm garment of myth. But the thorns tear the warm garment and the cold blasts penetrate through the rents, and the man who has become accustomed to its warmth suffers far more from these blasts than a man who has hardened himself to them from the first. Moreover, those who deceive themselves generally know at bottom that they are doing so, and live in a state of apprehension lest some untoward event should force unwelcome realisations upon them. (Russell, 1930/2006, p 171)

Knowledge enhancement and changing perceptions of the human condition occur without reference to whether or not they are likely to benefit individuals or society. They may even cause discomfort, such as the realisation of the falseness of earlier conceits of a human centric universe. Regardless of the consequences, movement in human thought is unstoppable in the longer, if not in the shorter, term. Nevertheless it is worthwhile to consider the possible benefits that may accrue in respect of a more realistic appraisal of the operation of morality, and certainly it is essential in respect of the proposal to create an analytical tool intended to enhance the interaction of morality and public policy. While others may pertain, two major areas of likely gain are the enhancement of *transparency and pre-emption* and the securing of more *timely and flexible public policy responses*.

Transparency and pre-emptive assessments

Amongst the benefits to be gained by an approach that involves ongoing review of developments within the moral sphere and their public policy interface, and which recognises the complexity of the moral function in accommodating impulses, is open, transparent engagement with the evidence. While this may be viewed as a sufficient good in itself, there are projected gains in terms of outcomes from this transparency. Open acknowledgement and understanding of the range of human impulses and behaviours would facilitate a more reflexive and coherent response than is currently in evidence. It has the potential to tip the balance of public policy more clearly in favour of a pre-emptive approach in respect of institutions and transactional relations. Here we flag up a sample of high profile administrative areas to make the case across finance, care and family policy.

Pre-emption in the worlds of finance and care

As noted earlier in the chapter, lack of pre-emption can be seen strikingly in finance. The temptation to a major and quick kill within the financial market is an integral part of its functioning to the substantive exclusion of other impulses, in particular those associated with the social instincts. The rush for gain with a blinkered momentum prior to the financial crash of 2007–10 was largely condoned by public policy. The ethos of turning a blind eye and operating with loose controls fuelled an environment that led to rule bending – followed by recrimination. Attitudes changed overnight to self-righteous blame, a volte-face predictably consequent on a failure to dispassionately consider the spectrum of human impulses and the way that they respond to particular social environments. The failure to pre-empt is habitual and consequently the resumption of business as usual, apart from some minor tinkering with the shoring up the credit worthiness of banks, until the next wringing of hands with horror was entirely predictable. Transparent acknowledgement of predicaments is preferable to an ethos of wilful blindness. Precautions that can be taken are more likely to become apparent against a backdrop of open assessment, and where they are not available or are rejected, there is in a transparent environment greater opportunity to prepare for possible negative outcomes. One might anticipate with such an approach a rather more serious discussion and engagement with different models of financial relations and expectations.

The revelation of gross inadequacy and cruelty within social care institutions, also described earlier in the chapter, provides a further case in point where the assessment of operations within a framework of open acknowledgement of human impulses and proclivities in particular situations, for example in respect of the vulnerable and dependent, would have had an ameliorating impact. Such transparency in respect of care would have enabled precautions to be adopted from the start, with systemic integration rather than a *post facto* hue and cry for judicial processes to be activated and for heads to roll, with precautions applied characteristically as sticking plaster.

Family policy

Some policy spheres have a particularly close association with morality – a direct interface where the subject is overtly addressed. One such is family policy analysed here by way of example. The case is made that there would be benefits from the proposed focus on a greater understanding of human behaviour and the management of tensions in familial relations rather than engagement with either sentimentality or outrage. It would entail a move away from exaggerated swings between a conceptualisation of family life as all about love to incantations of horror at the other end of the spectrum at the expression of individualism, selfishness and antagonism. Acknowledgement does not imply acceptance of the detrimental impingement of impulses on others. Rather the management of tensions based on an open recognition of their existence involves the weighing up of individual and collective needs and drawing protective human rights more closely into the moral sphere.

There are aspects of family policy where accumulated experience has prompted extensive monitoring and scrutiny, but there is still a lack of a fully pre-emptive approach addressing the range of impulses at play. Here we consider by way of illustration the critical issues of child abuse, adult partnership violence and elder care.

• Child protection and the identification of abuse have advanced considerably in the 20th century both conceptually and through better facilities. There is understanding of child abuse and the widespread risk of its occurrence with sophisticated professional engagement within social work geared to its detection and containment. Intensive work is being undertaken with children and their families. The apparatus installed has even been decried in some quarters as being over-elaborate and intrusive with exaggerated fears injected into everyday adult child relations. Much of this web of intervention has resulted from an incremental layering of controls in response to the anxieties following child abuse tragedies such as the cases of Victoria Climbié and Baby 'P' (Laming, 2003, 2009; Munro, 2011; Henricson, 2012). It has not, however, been prompted by a full understanding of the impulses in operation in adult–child relationships. Consequently there may indeed be an exaggerated response pursuant to highly publicised instances of child abuse, while at the same time there are aspects of habitual abuse that have received scant attention.

In relation to paedophilia, there have over the years been the odd vendettas against paedophiliacs, but, as previously discussed, no open acknowledgement of the endemic nature of the practice; and yet it must have been known to be prevalent at some level of consciousness, if not with a degree of complicity. The volume of paedophilia and its reach into the establishment has suddenly erupted into the social consciousness with a high profile public enquiry into historic child sex abuse being established amidst accusations of a cover up, alongside evidence of widespread current abuse practices in parts of the UK affecting thousands of children (Office of the Children's Commissioner, 2013). While there is much expression of dismay, we are still lacking a full and dispassionate appraisal of the emotions involved and their latent existence within the wider population.

The disciplining of children by their parents through assault – physical punishment – has been and continues in significant measure to be condoned. A blind eye is turned towards what, over the years, has been widespread practice. Where the movement towards recognising such common abusive behaviour for what it is has made any headway, it has been as a result of the evolving concept of rights – in this case children's rights – supported by instruments such as the United Nations Convention on the Rights of the Child 1989.

- A similar thrust of emerging rights' perspectives has prompted greater attention to domestic violence. As women have emerged from their position as men's chattels and have asserted their right to protection, coupled with material independence, domestic violence has been ratcheted up the law enforcement agenda (Crown Prosecution Service, 2015). As with child abuse, while there have been moves in favour of acknowledging the alter ego of family life, this has come as a consequence of rights' activation in which a human rights dimension features (Pinker, 2012) together with crisis exposures, for example from the work of Women's Aid and women's refuges – not as a result of considering the range of impulses in the round. Hence we have a continued saccharine perspective at the start of relationships and envisioning of family life. The absurdity of the continued marriage ceremony commitment for life in the face of the evidence is an obvious exemplar. Pre-emptive reflection and associated measures remain limited with *post hoc* retribution substantially the ongoing order of the day.

- Elder dependency within family life is a further sphere in respect of which the occasional waves have been made over violence, bullying and neglect; there is some, but seriously limited, awareness of elder abuse. The relationship between adult child and elderly parent suffers from a lack of definition in terms of public policy. The nature of familial responsibilities for the elderly remains largely untouched by the law, while social expectations affect only those children that are susceptible to such pressure (Deech, 2010; Henricson, 2012). This definition deficit in respect of families' obligations has transferred to the state's caring role where there is repeated failure to respond to the scale of need and to specify the scope of statutory obligation (The Law Commission, 2011; Commission on Funding of Care and Support, 2011). It is a question of coming clean about the degree to which society is prepared to commit to protecting the vulnerable. Feelings of compassion vie with reluctance, even resentment, over the burden of a dependent, redundant citizen. Avoidance of open recognition of the multiple contradictory impulses that engage the emotions in respect of the elderly has resulted in less than adequate care in many instances and physical and psychological abuse both within families and institutions.

The interplay across these dimensions of family life, the adult to child relationship and the adult to adult relationship, comprise an interconnected web of jostling motives. They encompass the multiple conflicting features of sexuality from the violent and sadistic to romantic transference, companionship and tenderness. Jealousy and damaged and enhanced identities have their sway. Material concerns feature; they range from material interdependence to desire for control; they include feelings of greed concerning inheritance and the spoils of divorce. Resentment over the burdens of care, obligation and unacceptable dependence exist alongside compassion and gratitude. These drives and more all co-locate within families. In real life multiple and conflicted impulses drive relationships that are not solely about compassion and the social instincts. Their fuller and more open and honest appraisal would facilitate facing up to and addressing the realities of family life; expectations in line with the actuality of behaviour may emerge and a more proactive accommodation ensue, with rights providing the essential protection. A critical component of this shift in perspective on family relations and consequential family policy is the recognition that behaviours that are currently treated as *exceptional* are in fact *habitual*. Shock and crisis management with a focus on retribution would be diminished in these circumstances in favour of a broader and rather more stoical overview of human behaviours.

In this discussion of the family sphere the protective nature of 'rights' has emerged. There are examples of where rights have had a protective role in relation to physical and mental abuse; they have operated in respect of material welfare and matters of identity, as well as with regard to violence. Human rights processes in the national and international sphere have grown in response to the atrocities of the Second World War. They are controlling devices to prevent abuse, not an aspirational tool to reach the realm of Nirvana. There have been grass roots components, particularly in relation to the protection of social groups such as women and children, alongside instruments of international law. They operate at the level of both individual and wider social relations. As one of the principal features of 21st-century philosophy of governance they deserve consideration as a significant potential tool in a model of morality concerned with the accommodation of impulses and their cultural overlay.

Timely and flexible public policy

A further major benefit envisaged from a fuller understanding of the role of morality in managing impulses is the enhancement of the capacity of public policy to respond flexibly and in a more timely fashion to shifts in social mores and moral perception within different cultural settings. There has been some recognition of the need for a reflexive public policy resource in respect of the moral precepts that apply to scientific developments with the establishment of the Emerging Science and Bioethics Committee. There are also examples of short-term inquiries considering the frontiers of specific ethical issues such as the Committee of Inquiry into Human Fertilisation and Embryology. The drawback with these various bodies is that they have a limited remit. The Equality and Human Rights Commission inevitably has a moral dimension, but from a limited protective civil rights perspective. The consequence of the fragmentary nature of these facilities has been a disorganised, inadequate statutory response to pressures for change in the moral sphere. Examples range from pressures in respect of personal relations and existential matters to questions about an inclusive approach to different strands of religious and secular commitment, through to concerns over material inequality.

Personal relations and existential matters

The dilatory, slow process of addressing the demand and necessity for change has been examined in detail in respect of assisted dying in Chapter One. A combination of a failing legal dimension with conspicuous flouting of the law, the imposition of high levels distress, the change in public attitudes and a highly articulate public debate over decades has still not generated full government engagement with the issue. It remains subject to highly publicised but ineffectual private members' bills in parliament. Delays followed a similar pattern of long-term campaigning in respect of the legalisation of abortion before a private members bill finally succeeded in liberalising the law in 1967; the Abortion Law Reform Association had been established in 1936. In the meantime the law was habitually flouted and the subterfuge resulted in distress and risk to health with secretive and backstreet abortions. The human rights dimension to the criminalisation of homosexuality and the suffering experienced as a result of its implementation is self-evident (Committee on Homosexual Offences and Prostitution, 1957). The continuation of this prohibition until partially lifted in 1967, despite constant transgression of an inoperable law and campaigns throughout the 20th century, is extraordinary from the perspective of 21st-century norms and equalities' legislation. As with abortion reform, the liberalising Sexual Offences Act 1967 relied on a private members' bill. Taking the legalisation of homosexual acts forward to establish full access to a family life for gay people through civil partnerships, marriage and the right to adopt has taken a further four decades, and providing access to civil partnership status for cohabiting heterosexual couples has still not been acceded to despite the implied infringement of human rights.

Responding to changes in religious and secular commitment

A major morality issue that has particular pertinence in a multicultural society is the functioning of religion and secularism in the public sphere. The challenge to the dominant role of the established church – the Church of England – has been conducted on many fronts over centuries. It has moved from the relationship with other Christian denominations to the current role of other faiths and that of secularism and humanism. The discrimination of a ban on a monarch with catholic affiliations is symptomatic of a slow, reluctant response to changed expectations – an astounding anachronism. There is no clarity on the eligibility of a declared non-believer to undertake the principal position of state, but the required oath to be the 'defender of the faith' implies an obligation to commit to the Church of England. The House of Lords, where matters of morality are debated from time to time and which has a considerable hold over matters such as the law on assisted dying, has places reserved for 26 bishops of the Church of England; no other religious or non-religious exponents of morality receive such preferential treatment. The Woolf Institute's Commission on Religion and Belief in British Public Life has questioned this situation and has put forward proposals to accommodate other religions in the upper chamber (Owen, 2015)

Piecemeal nods in the direction of inclusiveness in public life creep through in a haphazard, ill thought through fashion. Within education, for example, there is more leeway for the different faiths to exert influence. Coming not from a position of promoting inclusiveness or a considered proposition on the mode of addressing moral teaching amongst the young, the existence of schools of different faiths operating within the public sector has essentially been an *ad hoc* concession because of a precedent set by the role and public funding support acceded to Christian faith schools. Arguments of institutional fairness have pertained in an era when self-governing 'free schools' and parent power have also been advocated. Alongside this augmentation of faith schooling has been scant regard for large swathes of the population brought up in families with a secular ethos. For years subjected to a Christian dimension in education, latterly they have had access to teaching about a wider range of faiths in non-faith schools, but on the whole the curriculum underplays the humanist atheistic perspective (British Humanist Association, 2014b; 2015). Indeed the apparent intention of the government, subject to consultation, is to further reduce humanism and philosophy within the school curriculum with the teaching of two religions set to become the sole expectation (*Observer*, 2015). The benefits to be had from a broader, transparent and purposeful apparatus for the consideration of the fundamentals of morality and associated public attitudes are clearly demonstrated by this muddled education debacle.

Material inequality

One of the most sensitive and controversial areas at the interface between morality and public policy concerns the material and equality issues of fairness, redistribution, social security, welfare and taxation. This is undoubtedly a core political theme, but so too are issues around the regulation of personal relationships with social conservatism at odds with a liberalised stance. Core politics are not detached from national moral attitudes. The charging of government with a duty of providing itself with a focused and ongoing information resource concerning moral perspectives and their shifts facilitating flexibility and a coherent response does not suggest the eliciting of a particular government position. It is a matter of providing an informed springboard for the development of public policy, rather than determining that policy.

Looking at the recent past, there might have been benefits from taking a moral reading over changes to the welfare state, with a long held national consensus following the Second World War having been challenged and eroded by a piecemeal chipping away – a process that has taken place over the last four decades without overall appraisal of moral perspectives (Pierson, 1994; BBC, 2011; Bauer et al, 2012). Anxieties across the political divide over the implications of out of control inequality, an inequality that has mounted over time without serious challenge, are a further case in point where the monitoring of the moral underpinning to social transactions might have prompted an earlier, more coherent response (Dorling, 2014; Yellen, 2014; Elliot and Pilkington, 2015). Sustained and significant flouting of the intent of the law is another area where a morality overview might have alerted action earlier rather than *en retard*, as is currently the case with attempts to catch up with tax avoidance/evasion and other features of the market operating at full tilt.

The need for a morality litmus test

These examples and other areas of public policy embodying moral issues would have benefitted from a process that would have triggered an assessment of the moral fundamentals at stake and consideration of possible change in public policy responses. Inter-cultural, inter-generational and other potent moral tensions would have an enhanced opportunity for accommodation as a consequence of a fuller recognition of the significance of morality.

Overview

The argument in this chapter has tackled the implications, challenges and counterbalancing benefits of the book's proposition. That proposition has two closely aligned elements. The first comprises the establishment of a process for an ongoing overview of moral issues and pressures for change pertinent to public policy – an analysis resource – and the second, which should inform the first, is that morality is not solely geared to the promotion of the social instincts – and consequently a narrative of 'progress'; rather it is a tool for the management of diverse human impulses. Both of these contentions are controversial with potentially problematic consequences as they push against barriers of received thought and practice.

The latter – the move from progress to the management of impulses – presents a difficult expectation affecting, as it does, a deep-seated habit of perception and action. It detracts from the comfort of a progressive stance and the linked relegation of problems to the realm of the *exceptional* rather than the *habitual*.

Neither does it offer enlightenment progress lite *amelioration* as a means of holding onto a comforting mode of thought. The discussion rebuts a recoiling from the prospect of change and draws on historical examples of transition. It demonstrates that a realistic appraisal of human functioning, including the stasis of the human psyche – 'we are as we are' – does not imply a reactionary lens on social affairs. Rather open acknowledgement points to a more pre-emptive and flexible course of action with a predisposition to expect and address change within morality and its interface with public policy. This realistic model recognises the necessity for protection in the face of the implications of human impulses. It draws on the positive experience of the rights movements in terms of protecting the vulnerable and proposes some emulation.

The former – governmental review of moral issues – will undoubtedly provoke deprecating cries to the effect that morality and government do not mix and should be kept at arm's length – complaints of interfering nanny states, over-weaning power and more. To which the response must be that government and morality are inextricably linked, but currently by default and in an ill-informed, haphazard, change-shy and fumbling manner. The case for an enhanced resource to gauge movements and issues in the moral domain has been made in this chapter; the nature of that analytical tool and the feasibility of its operation are considered in the next.

FIVE

Managing morality:
a public policy analytical tool

The book thus far has made an argument supporting a more clearly framed, informed and creative conjoining of government and morality. It has made the case that government should no longer 'not do morality' in the same vein that Alastair Campbell, the New Labour public relations adviser, once said of his political masters that "We don't do God." Of course Campbell's assertion of the parameters of government was in many ways wise. The risk of alienating those who have a different stance in the stratosphere of belief systems and annoying an electorate sceptical of politicians with preaching and top down exhortations is real enough. But a reality check will flag up the following reasons for active government engagement in the moral sphere.

Government handles morality as of necessity; it is the very stuff of its existence as it legislates on criminal justice matters, family relations, scientific advances and indeed the panoply of socioeconomic relations. The question then is not whether it should engage with moral functions, but rather how it should do so. And this query is not about whether it should plump for this or that side in a moral tussle, but rather the mode of its considering the operation of morality's interface with public policy.

The current deficiency is one of sweeping the awkwardness of the term and its connotations under the carpet, avoiding questions of population attitudes and behaviour, and failing to get a full grasp of the issues. As a consequence the policy changes demanded by the natural and inevitable movement of social mores have been ill managed and delayed. The integration of cultural and conceptual differences has suffered as a result of this default route. The public has been ill served as government has waited for its hand to be forced, reliant on private members' bills and turning a blind eye to legal processes that are insouciant of need and behind the times.

The fraught and long drawn out divisive battles over the legalisation of homosexuality, abortion and assisted dying have all followed aspects of this trajectory as has the protection of children, women and the elderly from physical, mental and material abuse. Socioeconomic relations – wealth generation and distribution – have similarly borne the cost of a failure to flush out for discussion major changes in the direction of travel and their relationship with human impulses and protective needs. The examples that have been considered here are not exclusive, but they are poignant illustrations and typify the concerns of the UK in the 20th and 21st centuries.

The negative outcomes experienced in these examples have ranged from acute personal suffering to a society ill at ease with itself. A lack of perspective and understanding of the kaleidoscopic operation of morality and human behaviours has taken its toll. The acceptance of a hands-off approach generally endorsing a notion that things will nudge forward in an enlightenment direction has proved itself to be ineffective with the evidence of discordant, less than satisfactory outcomes. Offering a focused resource capable of considering these matters in the round would provide some opportunity for gaining a handle on issues that perplex to excess because they are not faced up to. It would not be a panacea for societal ills, but may offer a means of lessening some unnecessary friction as a consequence of increasing understanding of behaviours and intrinsic divergence and viewing the accommodation of the same as a laudable objective.

A further strand to the argument favouring the endeavours to establish a formal process bridging the morality and public policy divide relates to the proposed reshaping of the conceptualisation of morality. The proposed alteration of the 'terms of reference' for the relationship to one explicitly geared towards a conception of morality as the management of a range of conflicting and shifting impulses responding to cultural and material pressures constitutes an additional imperative for providing a facility to support collective reflection.

Numerous pitfalls could ensnare any proposition for a facility to enhance the synergy between morality and public policy. The dangers are multiple, ranging from a house of cards, a dreamer's elaborate edifice with the distinct possibility of being subject to ridicule, to a proposal suffering from a lack of definition, excessively diffuse in terms of the issues falling within its remit so as to constitute a meaningless enterprise. Producing a blueprint for a meaningful resource is the formidable task set for this chapter.

The intention is not to devise hard and fast recommendations, but rather to establish some options that could deliver opportunities for enhancing the morality and public policy relationship – to initiate discussion and purposeful consideration of a model capable of making a positive, significant contribution with the capacity for securing support in the world of practical operations. The experience of bodies with something of a similar remit will be reviewed to assist the process. Negative and positive consequences of past initiatives will be examined with an expectation that there will have to be tradeoffs in the devising of a model. The principal issues to be considered relate to the nature and scope of the morality to be included for assessment and the functioning mode of the resource. There is also a need to reflect on the interrelationship between a new comprehensive facility and institutions that currently have issues specifically defined as containing a moral dimension within their remit.

Questions to be addressed

Pertinent questions to be addressed span the following conundrums.

Morality is implicated in the operation of living at various levels. How can an institution both embrace the function of comprehensive analysis and set boundaries to its role in order to be operable and credible? Should there, for example, be a differentiation between morality of 'duty', largely associated with the law, and morality of 'aspiration', which encompasses a wider spectrum of behaviour? In responding to this question consideration would need to be given to the bearing each has on the other, with extra legal social custom exerting strong expectations and the line between duty and aspiration being blurred as a custom is drawn into or excluded from the legal sphere.

A further delineation might be drawn between morality which is principally concerned with matters of individual personal relationships and existential concerns, matters such as sexual conduct and its institutions, the sanctity or otherwise of life, and life and death choices that define humanity such as abortion, assisted dying, scientific manipulation – these and morality that is concerned with matters constituting the bread and butter of life, the operation of socioeconomic relations including the generation and distribution of wealth, health and opportunities for fulfilment. However linked the spheres may be, there is a perception of difference in the way the two are treated. The former are often deemed as off limits for the political fray; they are matters of conscience that are hermetically sealed – convenient enough for governments ducking and weaving the institution of policy change. The latter, because it is about the fight for resources, is instead the central ground of politics, the raison d'être of political parties. It is not treated preciously in the way that the former is; instead we have gloves off fighting between impulses. This depiction of two strands of moral reality is oversimplified, but it is an oversimplification that reflects current public policy responses to morality, and which certainly would need to be taken into account.

A further matter for reflection is the point at which the 'body' should activate its investigations. Should it keep an eye on the sea of morality including that which is in a state of settled consensus as well as aspects of morality and its interface with public policy that may be in a state of turmoil? Or should there be triggers for the focus of attention and, if so, what broadly should these be?

In terms of the resource itself, consideration would need to be given to the nature of its powers. While evidently the organisation would not be intended to undertake a decision-making function or to displace the role of the legislature, the scope of its conclusions would need to be determined – for example whether they should embody recommendations, what the force of those recommendations might be and whether the body should have a catalytic or purely analytical function.

The delineation and relationship of this comprehensive resource with other bodies with responsibility for some specific aspect of moral investigation, such as the Committee of Inquiry into Human Fertilisation and Embryology, would require attention. Questions of overlap and association would all arise. Most critically there would be a need to establish the relationship between such a body and the processes in operation to promote human rights. The relationship with the Equalities and Human Rights Commission would be a major point of reference necessitating consideration of both the conceptual and institutional interconnection between morality and protective human rights.

Duty and aspiration

There is general familiarity with the difference between 'aspiration' and 'duty'. *Aspiration* exists outside the legal system. Much of it comprises positive expectation and is tied into moral philosophy – the aspiration to lead a fulfilled life, to establish goals, to work hard, to extend a helping hand and more. It also relates to a person's inner life with sophisticated mechanisms for meditation and prayer. *Duty* in this context has a predominantly legal orientation and often has a negative slant to it – restrictions on behaviours, not to steal, assault, etc., although it also has a requirement to perform certain acts, for example to fill in tax returns and pay taxes, to care for children, to fight for country.

There are, of course, exceptions across the spectrum of this thematic divide. A brief set of illustrations is sufficient to make that case. In relation to tax there is a growing expectation within tax administration that affirmative action to pay taxes should be taken and that elaborate tax avoidance schemes should be eschewed; social pressure has been exerted to such a degree that, what might have been viewed as an aspiration, might now be classed within the legal side of the morality divide. *Mens rea*, the intention to commit an act, which is the requirement for guilt in most criminal justice cases, is an area where the inner life is subject to legal implications. Legislation around racial discrimination is a blurred and controversial field where speech and behaviour closely linked to attitudes have entered the world of criminal justice. When the crime of incitement of racial hatred was first introduced there were challenges as to whether it had overstepped the mark into the private sphere. Similar reservations were expressed with the introduction of the original anti race and sexual discrimination legislation. It was considered by some that the element of attitude in discrimination was too great to be able to be handled as a legal offence, and yet these provisions have survived and flourished. There are, too, many blurred lines in relation to family life where aspirations concerning private relationships enter the public sphere such as marriage, the upbringing of children and the like.

Particularly noteworthy in this blurring of the lines between public and private is the fact that attitudes and aspirations inform the development of public policy. Take, for example, the aspirations associated with material and spiritual wellbeing and the aspirations to fulfilment in education and within personal relationships – all of these are generated in the individual, private domain, but securing their delivery spills over into communal endeavour. Many people's search for fulfilment and attitudes to social obligation and individual expression determine public policy and ultimately legislation.

The transposition of this influence across the public domain is self-evident and does not require further extrapolation. Nevertheless, however interconnected the aspirational/private and public/legal domains may be and blurred the demarcation, there is a widely perceived difference as described at the opening of this section. Taking into consideration both interconnection and difference, the focus of a resource to support the morality and public policy interface should perhaps be primarily geared towards aspects of morality that have a potential public policy dimension, but this should also be coupled with a brief to keep an eye on pertinent attitudinal change; moral introspection pursued for its own sake would not be included within that brief.

Interpersonal/existential versus socioeconomic relations

As previously discussed, there is a perception that these two dominant themes within morality differ. The former is construed as falling within the category of ring-fenced morality. In common parlance, when morality is talked about pertaining to government it tends to exist within a life, death, reproduction, sex and religious bubble and is frequently viewed as being above the fray of politics. Of course moral references emerge more broadly across the political enterprise, certainly in respect of socioeconomic relations and the formulation of public policy. Gordon Brown's 'moral compass' pervading his pledge to redistribution and fairness is resonant here and many would place their whole political disposition and activity within a moral explanation. There is also much blurring. Sexual relations, for example, have a major material and socioeconomic component ranging from financial support and property distribution to social identity.

Nevertheless, there is a habit of differentiation that causes governments to allocate interpersonal and life/death decisions to the realm of 'personal conscience' in votes within parliament. Logically the remit for a resource to address the morality and public policy interface should be inclusive of the range of dimensions – both in terms of their compartmentalised requirements for such support and in relation to the interconnections. However, there may be a pragmatic decision to be made. Pressures towards thinking smaller scale may apply in the first instance and political realism and sensitivity may dictate a hands-off decision in respect of the socioeconomic sphere. A focus on the personal and existential dimension would be a feasible option.

Triggers

There are arguments to be made favouring an all in comprehensive operation across the static and changing aspects of morality, across synchronised and disjointed aspects of the morality and public policy interface. An ongoing review of this nature would provide a complete current picture and one that extends over time. Perspective and a fuller understanding of a rolling process of human intercourse would be the considerable return on such investment. But investment it would undoubtedly entail. The reality is that, in order to underwrite the selling value of this enterprise, there may be a need to hone in on particular pressure points that conspicuously demand attention.

Such triggers might include individually or severally:

- anxieties over discrepancies between legislation and behaviour sufficient to constitute moral friction;
- attitudinal change sufficient to cause a questioning of the status quo;
- material change such as scientific developments that have implications for existential matters of life, death, human identity and interpersonal relations;
- the significant need for a particular sector of society to receive greater protection in matters of individual or social relations.

These are not legalistic or hard and fast definitions, but are floated as possible indicators of the need for public policy changes. The decision to activate investigation and support would entail a degree of subjectivity and there would be instances of deserving causes falling through the net, but that is part and parcel of operations and a fallibility to be factored in. Elements of choice and the missing of pertinent issues would be inevitable, but falling short of the absolute should not preclude the attempt to reap the benefits to be garnered from making some headway in these matters.

It is noteworthy that the triggers do not necessarily imply changed behaviour as the point at which public policy requires alerting to a moral swell or discrepancy sufficient to merit attention. The proper prompt is rather more oriented around the movement and strength of attitudes – attitudes to the status quo as well as changed behaviours. This may suggest the necessity for keeping a low level tab on attitudes within the population – nationwide and within specific groupings. The British Social Attitudes Survey and numerous other surveys provide much data and should be the subject of scrutiny. Filling gaps in current data provision would also need to form part of the brief for a morality and public policy resource.

Powers

The powers of the resource will require tight definition. Of prime consideration must be its relationship with the legislature and the executive. As already highlighted, the body would not have legislative powers of any sort. The question nevertheless remains as to what relationship it would have with parliament and the civil service. Should it be located with either of these institutions or be external to government? Some of the feasible options are floated here for debate.

A parliamentary body

If a close connection with parliament were to be desired, one possibility would be for the resource to be a parliamentary body. In this scenario the constitutional classification of that body would be a critical issue. All Party Parliamentary Groups are informal bodies. Instigated by interested Members of Parliament (MPs), they are largely a location for external pressure groups and stakeholders to have a link with the parliamentary world, a platform for advocacy and the sharing of ideas. There can be no doubt that they do have a role to play in fuelling public debate, but they do not have the facility to commission reports with clout or to examine witnesses with the same degree of formality as a parliamentary Select Committee. The Select Committee alternative is an option that would have considerably more influence within parliament and in respect of the executive. It would have powers to summon and examine witnesses with full recording of proceedings and a substantial administrative support structure.

It is worthy of note that in terms of scope Select Committees offer the precedent of addressing broad subject matters on an ongoing basis. While the majority of Commons Select Committees shadow government departments, some have a role that crosses departmental boundaries such as the Public Accounts or Environmental Audit Committees. The breadth of their remit is substantial and fluid. The Public Accounts Committee, for example, has considered matters as diverse as global tax evasion, service provision, issues of inequality, and the scrutiny of particular public investments. Lords Select Committees do not shadow the work of government departments. Their investigations look into specialist subjects, taking advantage of the Lords' expertise and the greater amount of time available to them to examine issues. There are currently five major Lords Select Committees reflecting this breadth of purpose: the European Union Committee; the Science and Technology Committee; the Communications Committee; the Constitution Committee; and the Economic Affairs Committee.

The government responds to the findings of Select Committees and they have increasingly become vehicles with teeth to hold the executive to account. Drawing widespread media coverage, they have had a profound impact on public debate in recent times from the quizzing of the Murdochs over phone tapping by the press to the raising of the bar in terms of expectation of payment of tax by large global businesses that have taken the game of tax avoidance to anti-social extremes. There can be no doubt that if this model were to be adopted, the morality and public policy resource would be capable of having a major impact in terms of the wider conceptual public debate. It would also stand a good chance of influencing executive decisions facilitating and even forcing the consideration of issues along the morality–public policy interface that are currently skirted. Familiarity in formal settings has its own momentum with habit easing the process and the light of day exerting a degree of pressure. That is not to say that the findings of the Select Committees result in governments following the emergent recommendations, and that is as it should be – diffusion of power would be problematic in terms of democratic relationships with the electorate and certainly is not what is anticipated for this enterprise.

There may be deemed to be a risk that morality and public policy is too esoteric and expandable a topic for a parliamentary committee, but the evidence suggests otherwise, that in fact there is the committee capacity to undertake such a necessary sustained over-arching review. The broad span of operations of the Select Committee structure has been successful in moving public debate and in looking at issues with rather less blinkered vision than might be the case within the operational delivery function of government departments or groups of MPs scrutinising particular prospective legislation. Furthermore, as discussed, there remains the possibility of restricting the remit of a morality and public policy committee to issues of the personal and existential, excluding the socioeconomic dimension.

Commissions

A parliamentary committee offers the combination of a considerable influence over, and familiarity with, the operations of government and independence borne of a specific role of holding the executive to account. The question is how far would the location of the morality and public policy resource *outside* this framework be a match? Would it be more conducive to efficacy or less? Certainly placing the resource within a government department would be out of the question as it would then constitute part of the executive and so be critically hampered in terms of challenging government. Independent commissions and bodies outside the boundaries of both parliament and the civil service are plentiful with models of different shades of independence and clout on which to draw.

Commissions are frequently established around particular issues. Some of these are inquiries with a retrospective slant on a 'what went wrong' basis informing future practice to redress particular wrongs, for example the judicial public inquiry established in 2011 led by

Lord Justice Leveson into the culture, practices and ethics of the press following phone hacking scandals (Leveson, 2012). Further examples can be seen in the inquiries following concerns over substandard abusive care of the vulnerable in institutions, such as the judicial inquiry into child abuse in children's homes in Wales led by High Court judge Sir Ronald Waterhouse QC, which reported in 2000 (Tribunal of Inquiry into the Abuse of Children in Care in the Former County Council Areas of Gwynedd and Clwyd since 1974, 2000; *Telegraph*, 2012).

Other inquiries have a less blame, lessons to be learnt orientation, which might be considered to be rather more in tune with the aspiration for a morality and public policy resource. The Committee of Inquiry into Human Fertilisation and Embryology chaired by Mary Warnock, which reported in 1984, is one such example. The Committee was required 'to consider recent and potential developments in medicine and science related to human fertilisation and embryology; to consider what policies and safeguards should be applied, including consideration of the social, ethical, and legal implications of these developments; and to make recommendations'. It was a body that had considerable influence on future directions. The Committee's recommendations for regulation resulted in the establishment of the regulatory body the Human Fertilisation and Embryology Authority.

A similar morality geared operation was the Departmental Committee on Homosexual Offences and Prostitution under the chairmanship of Lord Wolfenden. This offers a spectacular example of how an official, disinterested inquiry can produce recommendations that are completely ignored by government. The Wolfenden inquiry recommendation for the legalisation of private homosexual activity was shelved (Committee on Homosexual Offences and Prostitution, 1957). It is tempting to cite examples such as this as a reason for abandoning the route of official inquiries. On the positive side of the argument, however, it does appear that Wolfenden's recommendation assisted longer-term pressure for change. Its insights were frequently cited and were drawn on for the formulation of the 1965 Sexual Offences Bill to legalise private homosexual acts by its sponsors Leo Abse MP and Lord Arran (Abse, 1966).

An important consideration associated with shelved recommendations is the nature of one-off inquiries. With task completed, there is little chance of comeback in the face of government sensitivity and ducking of the issues. An ongoing review body on the other hand has sufficiently longevity to be able to nag. Such a nagging function would not usurp the legitimate democratic powers of government, but it would keep critical questions alive in the government and public's eye. This suggests that the principal focus in terms of precedent for the purpose of developing a morality and public policy resource should be on bodies that have a sustained rather than a single-issue, time-limited function and modus operandi. Prime examples are the Law Commission and the Equalities and Human Rights Commission. Both of these bodies have elements of interconnect with the morality–public policy divide and, through ups and downs, have survived and continue to have a purchase on public policy. Their operational models are summarised here as a point of reference for the development of an operable resource with the capacity to deliver value.

The Law Commission

The Law Commission was created by the Law Commission Act 1965 and the Law Commission Act 2006 to keep the law under review and to recommend reform where it is needed. The aims of the Commission are:

- to ensure that the law is as fair, modern, simple and as cost-effective as possible;
- to conduct research and consultations in order to make systematic recommendations for consideration by parliament; and
- to codify the law, eliminate anomalies, repeal obsolete and unnecessary enactments and reduce the number of separate statutes.

The Law Commission reviews areas of the law that have become unduly complicated, outdated or unfair. Following a process of research and consultation, the Commission makes recommendations for reform of the law to government.

Law reform projects

The Commission consults widely when establishing new programmes of law reform projects. It also takes referrals from government departments with the Lord Chancellor deciding the final contents of a law reform programme. The following criteria are deployed in determining an area of law for review:

- importance – the extent to which the law is unsatisfactory, and the potential benefits from reform;
- suitability – whether the independent non-political Commission is the most suitable body to conduct the review; and
- resources – valid experience of commissioners and staff, funding available, and whether the project meets the requirements of the programme.

Once the Law Commission has agreed to review an area of law the remit of the project is decided, in conjunction with the relevant government department. A study of the area of law is undertaken and its defects identified. Other systems of law are examined to see how they deal with similar problems. A consultation paper is issued setting out in detail the existing law and its defects, giving the arguments for and against the possible solutions and inviting comments. The paper is circulated widely to all interested individuals and organisations, and to the media. A report is then submitted to the Lord Chancellor and relevant secretary of state, giving final recommendations and the reasons for making them.

Organisation and status

There are five commissioners drawn from the legal profession and the chairman is either a High Court or an Appeal Court judge. They are appointed by the Lord Chancellor and the Secretary of State for Justice. The commissioners are supported by a chief executive, members of the Government Legal Service, parliamentary counsel, and research assistants.

Although closely associated with government, the Commission sets considerable store by its independence. It is a statutory independent body – an advisory, non-departmental public body sponsored by the Ministry of Justice. (Law Commission, 2015)

Equality and Human Rights Commission

The Equality and Human Rights Commission was established by the Equalities Act 2006 with a brief to challenge discrimination, and to protect and promote human rights.

The Commission describes its vision in the following terms.

- Our vision: We live in a country with a long history of upholding people's rights, valuing diversity and challenging intolerance. The Equality and Human Rights Commission seeks to maintain and strengthen this heritage while identifying and tackling areas where there is still unfair discrimination or where human rights are not being respected.
- Our mission: A catalyst for change and improvement on equality and human rights.
- Our roles: outcomes-focused strategic regulator, promoter of standards and good practice, authoritative centre of intelligence and innovation, and trusted partner. (Equality and Human Rights Commission, 2015)

Organisation and status

The Commission comprises nine commissioners drawn from across the human rights and equalities spectrum. It operates with a chair, a chief executive and support staff. While accountable to government and parliament, the Commission is independent having been established as an 'arm's length independent body' (Equality and Human Rights Commission, 2015)

A possible scenario that might be mooted would be for the morality and public policy resource to be attached to one or other of these ongoing commissions. Undoubtedly piggy backing in this way would offer comparative ease of administration. However, there may be anxieties that the particular focus of both initiatives would skew the roving brief of a morality function with its particular openness to change and different forces within society and the human psyche. The Law Commission may be viewed as having too great a legal focus delving into the intricacies and discrepancies of the operation of legislation. Nevertheless it must be said that it could have a relevant take on points of friction between behaviour and the law. The Equality and Human Rights Commission is focused on a cause, and though as a protection tool for the vulnerable it would undertake a role in relation to the morality and public policy perspective proposed in this discussion, that should only form a part of the project; an add on arrangement with the Equality and Human Rights Commission in the lead position may draw attention away from the broader, detached scope of the morality and public policy enterprise. A preferred approach might be to draw on these models in developing a separate, stand alone, ongoing commission.

Academia and think tanks

An altogether different route would be to treat the morality and public policy facility as an arm's length, softer source of information. This would be would be in the vein of academic and think tank services. These operations have influence, but are considerably more diffuse and dependent on contributing to a pick and mix group of inputs into policy. Within academia there are undoubtedly umbrella programmes of the sort envisaged for the morality and public policy resource. 'Wellbeing' has come into vogue in recent years with the establishment of funding streams such as the Economic and Social Research Council's Health and Wellbeing programme. Wellbeing commentary can range over topics of sufficient breadth to be comparable to the stretched brief of morality; it encompasses physical, social, economic and psychological domains (Wollny et al, 2010).

There is independence in this approach, but it should be noted that the operations of academia are somewhat constrained by government funding, and can be influenced by the direction of that funding. It is a subtle control, but inevitably extant as universities have to bid for project finance within funding streams. A small example can be seen in the Thatcher era when sociology became the subject of derision as a hot air commodity and the role of social policy, by way of contrast, became enhanced as a practical worthy enterprise. Of course public bodies are dependent on government for funding. The difference lies in the pathway of withdrawal. The establishment of a funding stream for a particular area of research is rather easier to modify or redirect and, where there are time-limited features to the grant, closure is an easy option. For established bodies within public administration with a particular policy purpose, such as the Law Commission, disestablishment is rather more difficult. Reshaping is an option, but it draws public attention and protest as occurred with the amalgamation of the various equalities bodies into the Equality and Human Rights Commission in 1994 (Hope, 2010; Pegram, 2011). Nothing precludes disestablishment, but action may be deterred because of the public glare.

The influence of academia within policy is a long process of osmosis. There are instances where a particular finding may be seized on and given the light of public policy day by some government department or politician or by the media, but this is not a reliable trajectory albeit that most funding invitations have policy influences as one of their criteria for successful applications.

Think tanks are rather more successful in making an impact relative to the volume of research undertaken; they have a disproportionate influence compared to academic institutions. Thus, for example, the Institute for Public Policy Research produced the report of the Commission on Social Justice (1994), which became a launch pad for the New Labour project. With less of a political bias and rather more in line with the proposals for a morality and public policy resource would be the Institute for Fiscal Studies, which commands respect as a disinterested body offering high level, pertinent research and expertise with a direct purchase on the business of government.

Way forward

With the criteria of independence and influence to the fore, this overview of institutional models suggests two leading options, a parliamentary Select Committee or an ongoing commission drawing on the experience and operational methods of the Law Commission and the Equality and Human Rights Commission. Both models are able to make recommendations commanding attention.

A third possibility would be a take on the think tank approach following the Institute for Fiscal Studies. In terms of constitutional strength, organisational robustness and capacity to resist the slings and arrows of a turbulent political fray, the leading options are to be preferred, but the Institute of Fiscal Studies approach is a worthy second best.

Human rights

A significant component of a public policy response to morality as the management of fluid impulses must be the provision of a protective facility. Discussion in the previous chapter has alluded to human rights as offering a precedent for such a facility in respect of women and children's vulnerability. The argument favouring a rights dimension is that it constitutes an appropriate response to a realistic appraisal of the operation of social relations, an appraisal that is not reliant on the misconception of the dominance of the social instincts. The rights movement in its various guises has prompted recognition of some of the operation of human impulses that it might have been preferable to ignore or underestimate in a model that conceives a progressive, elevation of the social instincts view of life. This tendency has been discussed in relation to domestic violence and child abuse. The necessity for protection pertains across the equalities agenda in respect of the treatment of, for example, different genders, age groups, ethnic and cultural groups, people of different sexual orientations and those with disabilities. It pertains in respect of the operation of institutions vis-à-vis the individual and across the vulnerabilities identified in the European Convention on Human Rights involving inter alia the right to life, security and liberty of person, the right to a fair trial, the right to freedom of thought, conscience and religion, the right to respect for one's private and family life and the prohibition of discrimination, torture, forced labour and inhuman or degrading treatment.

Rights are a critical backstop to flush out and redress the consequences of unfettered power and impulse that operate to the detriment of the vulnerable. They would provide a counterbalance to the danger of the relativity of a culturally determined accommodation of impulses within different moralities. Thus behaviours and identities concerning gender, parent child relationships and elder care undoubtedly vary within different cultural settings in the UK. This may be tolerated and accommodated within the context of and with the proviso of protective human rights' limits.

Clearly, as with any instrument of social regulation, human rights are also the product of culture. However, despite being subject to influence in this way, they constitute the most significant moral bridge available within a multicultural society; in relation to these rights the cultural influence is international with human rights tenets broadly accepted as appropriate across the globe. They offer the validation of internationally accepted principles on which to build a framework of protection (Henricson and Bainham, 2005; Henricson, 2007). The incorporation of human rights within the morality and public policy resource is proposed. It would not usurp the role of the Equality and Human Rights Commission, but would rather operate in a complementary fashion.

Stakeholders

The question of stakeholders is a fraught one. There are arguments that there should be maximum ownership and participation in a morality and public policy resource by all stakeholders engaged in the development of morality in the UK – religious and anti-religious movements, pressure groups concerned with a particular moral stance lobbying for change or maintenance of the status quo, political parties and more. There are, however, weighty counter-arguments favouring a cautious approach to creating a participatory facility. The nature of advocacy of particular philosophies or causes is that the more vocal predominate leaving the non-participatory populous at a distinct disadvantage. For a research and analysis resource with the aspiration to influence, not from a particular position derived from conviction or cause, but from a position of as full an understanding as possible of the issues while searching for accommodation, a more detached option may be preferred. Such a detachment would mirror the operational approach of the parliamentary Select Committees and the commissions established for particular investigative purposes. The choice of the membership of the body would need to be weighed carefully to create as much balance and detachment as is feasible. The collation and analysis of evidence would need to be to the highest scientific standard.

Overview

The case made in the preceding four chapters has been for a reconceptualisation of morality embracing elements of universalism and relativity. The universalism relates to a definition of morality as the means by which impulses in the human psyche are accommodated both within the individual's internal world and in social relations ranging from personal affairs to collective socioeconomic functions. The relativistic aspects of morality relate to how such accommodation is influenced by a combination of material pressures and experience within a particular life and culture. The protection of the vulnerable in this melee has been conceived in this chapter in terms of the role of human rights. This constitutes a departure from a model that presupposes the predominance of the social instinct impulse with morality as the tool for securing such dominance.

With a model of morality somewhat divergent from currently broadly received notions, there is the need for consideration to be given to the support process required to promote understanding and an effective interface between morality and public policy. That requirement pertains both because of this reframing of expectations to be rather more in step with the reality of moral purpose, and because there has been a dislocation between morality and public policy over decades. The discomfiture associated with the nature of moral flux and perceived sensitivities has caused governments to engage in tactics of avoidance. Changes to public policy reflecting changing behaviours and attitudes have consequently been tardy and ineffectual. Embracing the fluidity of morality rather more 'full-on' as the business of government necessitates a facility to prompt and inform.

This chapter has endeavoured to consider options for such a facility. There has been an assessment of the remit and scope of the resource. Content wise the need for research has been identified in respect of population behaviours, attitudes and the functionality of current legislation in terms of both shifts and stasis in morality, with triggers to instigate in depth analysis in relation to identified pressure points. Two options have been put forward for debate in respect of the nature of the morality to be addressed: one being limited to personal relations and life/death existential matters; and the other, of greater breadth, encompassing in addition the morality of socioeconomic affairs. In terms of powers it has been proposed that, as well as providing ongoing review, the facility should have the potential for influence, making recommendations that carry weight. Institutional models capable of securing this end have been explored. Varying degrees of influence have been gauged and a short list of options drawn up each offering the potential for influence, but differing in terms of potency – a parliamentary Select Committee, an ongoing independent commission or a high level think tank.

The analysis has not produced hard and fast recommendations for a particular constitutional and institutional model, and, in terms of the scope of morality to be addressed, two possibilities have been offered, one fully comprehensive, one less so. The rationale for this reticence has been the intention to stimulate debate on these issues in response to the profound nature of the step being taken. There is the need for acclimatisation and consideration of the sensitivities and practicalities of building a supporting consensus.

SIX

Conclusion

This thesis has come a long way; it has crossed a discursive divide between the esoteric ravages of religious conflict, the belief and disbelief friction and an increasing biological interpretation of moral dispositions – to a consideration of the efficacy or otherwise of parliamentary committees, commissions, think tanks and academia. On the way it has traversed a minefield of commitment and critique of metaphysical and philosophical interpretation – elements of commonality and relativism and the morality of divergent human impulses ranging from the violent to the caring. And yet, for all the scale of the leap, there is a distinct and carefully plotted train of thought the destination of which is identified in the rationale for the book in the opening chapter, namely the deficient relationship between morality and public policy. Exploring that deficiency has involved a reappraisal of the nature of morality – a change of paradigm reflecting understandings and perceptions as they have emerged in the 21st century and consideration of what that necessitates. It has led to consideration of the practicalities – the mundane, but essential business of administration and ways of enhancing the capacity of government to respond to, rather than evade, the shifting sands of moral reflection.

What the thread of that argument does not do is engage in an exercise of breast beating, bemoaning the decline of morals. It does not do so either in the private or public sphere. In its preoccupation with the morality and public policy disconnect, it is not concerned that policy does not follow a particular moral precept or that it lacks a moral compass operating without conviction. It is more dispassionate and detached than any of these stances that frequently pepper political rhetoric and the opinion pages of the press. Rather it embraces and addresses the full scope of morality from a position of neutrality – recognising differences in moral perspectives and the role of morality as an accommodator of impulses, perplexingly varied in their nature.

It is from this position that the argument does bemoan the incapacity of public policy to respond in a way that may best facilitate what is a highly complex phenomenon. Morality is typified by cultural difference as well as common points of reference. It is inherently in a state of flux as cultures and material pressures mutate. Enhancing the capacity of public policy to habitually and readily absorb the concept of moral change into its administrative vocabulary is the objective – to articulate it rather than shuffling responsibility off to the preserve of the private conscience.

The book's raison d'être derives principally from a current predicament, although it has a pertinent historical context that the book also assesses. By and large those current circumstances that draw attention to the moral sphere were not anticipated in the recent past. They emerged after a period in the 1960s and 1970s when such issues tended to be side lined into the backwater of a passé naivety. That is not to say that ground breaking moral steps were not taken – indeed they were, albeit often belatedly, with legislation on equalities, race relations, homosexuality, abortion, the abolition of the death penalty and more. But morality as a concept, an abstraction at the forefront of the societal mind was absent. Moral philosophy, for example, had taken a dive as 'logical positivism' and the understanding of the operation of language and its relationship to thought came to the fore (Ayer,1936). Materialism of one sort or another was also firmly planted as a negative interpretation of Western society, on the one hand, and as an endorsement of growing wealth and a get rich quick credo, on the other.

In the latter part of the 20th century and the early 21st century these perceptions became not displaced but overlaid with a vocal religiosity and fundamentalism. The assertion of a metaphysical ethos was largely fuelled by a rejection of modernity and by the decline of socialism as a belief system in material redemption for disadvantaged individuals and societies. The metaphysical has not, however, had a free rein, certainly in world political terms, but also in terms of the movement of ideas with a radical secularism emerging and asserting its validity in an era when the religious voice has become deafening. Mutual resentment and recrimination have ensued. Morality, closely entwined with both sides, has pervaded the cacophony of belief and disbelief. Within the UK this divide has been reflected in a high profile standoff between secular and religious influences in the public policy sphere.

This has coincided with advances in scientific understanding of the operation of the emotions and associated behaviour. There is, however, a mix in operation between culture and given biological pre-dispositions that keeps the morality tussle alive – and beliefs are beliefs are beliefs. For all the scientific advances, there is a melee of perceptions that are strident in their assertions and counter assertions. In the search for solutions, writings on the subject have tended to mirror specific directions of moral and spiritual perception. Thus we have had anti-religious discourse of the like of Dawkins (1986; 2006) and pro religious retaliations (McGrath and McGrath, 2007; Jha, 2006). Even within the scientific domain there is a tendency to impose a particular solution drawn from a prejudicial viewing angle of the brain and behaviours. Consequently one sees a preoccupation with the capacity for empathy to the detriment of sufficient acknowledgement of a host of other impulses and their accommodation within ritual, culture and morality. There are, too, examples where neuroscience is endorsed, but is then sidestepped with arguments from moral philosophy being used in the search for ultimate single solutions. In the case of Greene (2014) we see a neuroscientist having recourse to utilitarianism as the overriding moral disposition geared, not to the brain's immediate reaction to stimuli, but to its cognitive process. Yet there is no substantive evidence that utilitarianism – securing the happiness of the greatest number – constitutes the 'solution' to which the moral mind aspires. Many other cogitated outcomes are a possibility from human rights to the promotion of the select, a gifted elite for example, or simply the imperative of personal fulfilment, for example in respect of creativity or sex or power. What is missing from the discourse – and indeed which may be contributing to the slide into one-angle theses on morality – is a broad overview of moral thinking in the 20th and 21st centuries. It is a gap that this book has sought to fill with a view to providing a formulation from which to construct a more adequate public policy response to morality in a multicultural society with a fast changing profile.

The gap relates not only to an appreciation of morality, but also to the interrelationship of morality with public policy. Muddled, one-sided thinking has contributed to a lack of understanding of the habitual state of flux in morality, and evasion of that troublesome phenomenon has led to a failure to respond suitably and in a timely facilitative way to moral pressures for public policy change. Morality is about the imposition of order on the chaos of impulse, not it seems in order that one impulse predominates, but rather to provide an accommodation that makes individual and social living manageable. It is about order, but in different cultural contexts. It involves both cultural stability and cultural movement, and it has a strong social impact. As such it necessitates engagement by those responsible for the development and administration of public policy. It requires a conscious handle on the moral sphere that is capable of responding flexibly to shifts in social mores, while at the same time sustaining a degree of continuity in order that society does not experience the shock of having the rug pulled from beneath its feet.

There has been a somewhat cowardly continued relegation of morality to a low-key, socially conservative establishment church, divorced from the majority of the population, but still with something of a sclerotic hold on aspects of government. There has consequently been a vacuum in the morality–public policy interface that this book has sought to remedy. In its attempt to do so it has considered morality across the history of thought and scientific development. Themes of division and coherence have been addressed in accordance with their relevance to the responsibilities borne by public policy.

Revelation and rationalism

Prominent in the public policy and morality profile must be the division between revelatory thought systems and humanistic rational ones. The tensions on this front are intense with resentment spanning belief systems, framing political states and fostering a negative perception of a degenerate, materialist West, through to an anti-religious constituency harbouring resentment over a perceived over-powerful religious lobby.

That is the circumstance of the division, but the content of the division is also highly pertinent to public policy formulation. The former, the revelatory category, grounds its moral structures in revelation. Consequently it is on the face of it, and indeed to a considerable degree in reality, less likely to be able to endorse changes in moral standards or behaviours. That said there are complexities in the composition of revelatory moralities that mirror and even accommodate a wide range of human impulses and indeed reflect human living in religious narrative and other social and artistic expressions. The revelatory mode varies enormously including, as it does, perspectives where there is a highly literal, personalised god through to world explanations cast more in terms of a life force, the latter being rather less dogmatic than the former.

The humanistic rational approach contrasts with the revelatory through its grounding of a moral system in rational thought – a cognitive construct rather than a view of morality as the product of an extra-human influence. Human fulfilment, whether individual or collective, is the objective. Within this model a thousand flowers bloom with broad thematic divides between the individual and the collective; the optimist and the pessimist; and between the absolutist advocating deontology – having set a moral code and sticking to it – and an outcomes endeavour, consequentialism – judging an action by its effects. Key traditions derive from Aristotle's realisation of human capacities, Rawls' individual goals, Kant's universal set of rules and duties, Bentham's utilitarianism, Marx's materialism and more. There are human rights, and we have seen Levenstein's synthesis of deontology and consequentialism in the context of human rights and utilitarianism. Each concept has been challenged, refined and merged within logical tortuous arguments across the wide-ranging enterprise of moral philosophy.

Revelation and rationalism are by no means wholly mutually exclusive. Moral philosophical arguments are frequently used within an overall framework of revelation. Undoubtedly revelatory systems tend to social conservatism – adherence to 'god given' edicts that are hard to shift in zinc with shifts in social mores. There are, however, divisions between traditional strands of metaphysical belief systems and elements that embrace a considerable degree of rationalism and, indeed, see aspects of their belief as metaphorical with morality determined in the human image. Examples are drawn in the discussion from both Islam and Christianity. In terms of rapprochement, it is also noteworthy that the secular field does not hold all the rational cards. There are secular models that have channelled understanding of human behaviour into motivational forces, such as self-interest, sex and power, that do not reflect the breadth of living experience. Theories of socioeconomic relations and political persuasions similarly buy into a selective dimension from which flexibility and a capacity for moderation are missing as reflected in some atheistic states. Communism is the exemplar here in terms of the recent past. A similar single-minded emotional commitment can be witnessed in some quarters in respect of the contrasting theory and credo of capitalism – most recently neo-liberalism. The role of tribalism exists within this scenario and across the revelatory secular divide. It has its own impetus of no mean proportions. Identity within tribal constructs pervades class, nationalism, ethnicity, religion and institutions. It is highly emotional and tenacious. It is perhaps tribalism, with its momentous entrenched hold, that presents the public policy and morality interface with its greatest challenge.

There is a split in terms of aspirational and observational philosophy – what people should do versus what they in fact do – across revelatory and rationalist perspectives that it is also important to acknowledge. These elements, often intertwined and mistaken one for the other, thread their way through the canon.

The various differences in approach across the reach of moralities and their philosophies, for all the attempts at reconciliation, remain in situ to this day and constitute the stuff with which public policy has to contend. One cannot say that one or other has won or indeed that a synthesis has emerged. Rather it seems from a retrospective glance across the spectrum that each has made a contribution of worth and validity within the parameters of what it is deducting from a point of principal or observation.

Commonality

The attempt to draw a common element from morality has been substantive and historical stretching back to Socratic belief in a common moral universe within which rational argument would be expected to result in agreement. Rational self-interest has been the unitary feature propounded by the likes of Descartes and Leibniz. Some discourse has deemed single emotions such as power lust to be the determinant of behaviour and lurking behind morality. Empathy is an emotion that has been perceived as at the root of morality by philosophers such as Hume and more recently by observational biologists such as Darwin, and has been associated with progressive expectations of humanity.

It seems that the search for commonality has in effect been the aspiration to impose a single perspective across the board. It is a belief in a unitary solution that fails to take account of the breadth of human impulse dynamics. And where there is acknowledgement of the complexity of the human psyche, as for example within Darwin's explanation, the model is one of questionably isolating a particular motive as dominant. Darwin's contention that morality is about managing impulses that run counter to pro-social behaviour is, it is suggested, flawed; management geared to securing long-term satisfaction is equally applicable to a range of non-empathetic impulses around individual fulfilment.

Relativism

The embrace of the breadth of moral perspectives comes rather less from arguments engaged in the pursuit of commonality – in effect single solutions – and rather more from relativism. Relativism, often decried as a quagmire of moral licence, has to recommend it the voice of liberalism and tolerance (Mill, 1859); there is also an element of resignation to the impossibility of reconciling difference. Strawson (1974) perhaps comes closest to the proposition posited here that within moral philosophy and wider commentary on the human condition there are 'truths but not truth' – perspectives hold good within their own terms of reference.

Relativism has taken hold in an era that is witness to moral turbulence in the form of growing individualism, flourishing cheek by jowl with cultural difference and pressures to shift moral perspective; much of this is the spin off of education, enhanced communication and the movement of populations. The dangers of the quagmire referred to are real enough and spotted by philosophers such as Mary Midgley (1984).

Scientific advances

Has scientific enhancement of our understanding of the moral brain counterbalanced slippery relativism? Following biological investigation and neuroscience are we on firmer ground? Certainly Darwin's detailed observations of the functioning of species and the operation of impulses are pertinent as are more recent neurological findings locating the span of impulses in different parts of the brain and a cognitive function associated with their order and accommodation. This is the essence of the commonality in morality that does exist – that morality is about ordering. But it is not necessarily about the imposition of one emotion over others; there is fluctuation and variation. The question is not whether these emotions exist, but what the upshot of their interaction is – and that has not been resolved by science. There are multiple unquantifiable pressures outside the biological, including cultural, material and individual experiences, that exert influence.

In relation to neuroscience, the location of an ordering of the impulses within the prefrontal cortex does not indicate which impulses are to be preferred or in which order. The case is made in this discussion that morality is about the management of a spectrum of emotional and cognitive pulls within the human psyche, with the social instincts being one, but not necessarily the dominant pull.

Shifts in morality demonstrate that there is evident capacity to reorder the management of the impulses – witness the changes in the role of individualism and collectivism, family duties, sexual mores, the treatment of death, matters of social deference and equality, tendencies in responding to the 'other' – levels of inclusion or exclusion across cultures, genders, sexual persuasion, social groups – and more. Indeed the differences in morality itemised here, as well as being evident from changes over time, are further exemplified in the differences that exist between cultures and individuals. This degree of differentiation throws into question any notion of biological pre-ordering. The function of religion in accommodating impulses from sadism to social oppression alongside support for caring and individual expression also points to a less than unidirectional role for morality.

We have then the grounding for morality in biological roots identified through scientific investigation. That grounding offers a commonality of purpose for morality – it being to accommodate the jostling host of impulses. This is coupled with shifting, multi-layered and different cultural, material and other influences on human thought and behaviour – a synergy with relativism. There are common and contrasting themes, synergies and tensions that demand attention, with rationalism and emotionalism intertwined across the piece. The development of a cohesive response demands an ongoing probing of and living with these phenomena.

Challenges and benefits

There are challenges and benefits in this interpretation that have to be borne in mind, not in determining its validity, but which are necessary to acknowledge in engaging with its practical application. The undermining of an enlightenment sentiment, the expectation of progress, is perhaps the most difficult issue to address. However much commentators contend that enlightenment perspectives have been shredded by a decline in the belief in the capacity of society to reform, they still hold sway, and Darwin's supremacy of the empathetic has something in common with a social belief system in progress. Certainly 'progress', aspiring to perfection rather than more realistically managing tensions, has maintained a hold on public policy thought. Resentment in respect of doubt in this regard can be seen in the reaction given to philosophers who have questioned the credentials of progress. Feelings run deep, but they are not insuperable. There are numerous examples from the past of dual belief systems operating following the emergence of new scientific perspectives on the human psyche and the universe – a residual emotional attachment alongside an intellectual recognition of an intellectual truth. The challenge is considerable – to sever an attachment to the notion of progression that so permeates our public policy language and way of handling social life. To date there has been a lack of alternative models of social living. Such an alternative is put forward here, guardedly, but with anticipation of potential gain.

The discussion has noted the benefits of orientating public policy towards a more realistic appraisal of the human condition. It has flagged up the possibility of a more pre-emptive approach being adopted as a consequence, and the gains to be had thereby.

It has examined both material and caring social relations in this regard. A repetitive surprise syndrome has been identified and construed as part and parcel of a delusory addiction to expectations of progress and a failure to embrace human motives and behaviours as they are. This is exemplified to a major degree in the love hate, sentimental and conflicted nature of family relations and policy responses thereto, with child abuse and paedophilia in particular projected as exceptional rather than endemic; responses are of outrage and dismay rather than adequate, measured pre-emption. Within adult couple relationships, too, the endemic nature of violence has taken rights' movements to start to flush out. And with elder care operating at the level of both family and state, feelings of compassion vie with resentment over the burden of a dependent, redundant family member and citizen; inadequate facilities, planning and regulation are the upshot of a failure to acknowledge this truth. Complementary and contradictory emotions – loves, hates, jealousy, the assuaging of loneliness, the nurturing of identities, material needs and greed – the full panoply of motives are the stuff of family life and wider social relations.

Critically the essential move is towards recognising that behaviours that are currently treated as *exceptional* are in fact *habitual*. Shock and crisis management would then give way to a broader, more stoical overview of human motives and behaviour. And this more honest appraisal and fuller understanding would fuel more informed, flexible and timely public policy.

The swap of the progressive narrative for impulse and tension management does not imply a socially conservative prognosis for public policy – rather the reverse. It implies a predisposition to facilitate change where that is emerging as the requirement of shifts in social mores. And the capacity to address change is critical. The discussion has probed examples of the detrimental impact of 'head in the sand' inflexibility on matters such as assisted dying, sexual orientation, abortion, the role of belief systems in the public sphere, caring and the issue of material inequality – diverse examples across the contemporary canvas of concerns.

The need for an ongoing review of the juncture between morality and public policy is the other principal contention in this thesis. It is not as radical a proposal as the move to recognise an impulse management morality function, but it is contentious in a sphere where the public–private divide carries its own baggage of sensitivity. That sensitivity is worth addressing and overcoming, as it has been in the past in respect of matters such as race and gender discrimination. Sustaining an overview of moral issues and pressures for change pertinent to public policy would undoubtedly contribute to rectifying current deficits in responsiveness and facilitate a closer alignment between society as defined by its moralities and public administration; it is worth doing.

Implementation

Equipped with these conclusions, the discussion then changes gear to assess the essential 'what and how' of such an overview. Following an examination of public inquiries of limited duration and more permanent institutions, the thesis concludes that an ongoing, broad function is required in order to achieve impact. Furthermore a morality and public policy body should be linked to government, but independent of it. Operating within these parameters some options are put into the frame for future debate. They encompass a parliamentary approach – the Select Committee – that might indeed be optimal, but optimistic as a first step. External, but government-initiated, commissions, such as the Law Commission and the Equality and Human Rights Commission, are also presented as viable. Further removed from government, but nevertheless influential, would be an approximation to the respected think tank, the Institute for Fiscal Studies.

Pragmatic choices would also need to be made in respect of the nature and reach of the moral issues to be surveyed. While the full breadth of moral thought is pertinent to understanding the operation of moral trends, it is concluded that the focus of a public policy overview should be on aspects of morality that have a potential public policy dimension.

The question is also posed as to whether or not the morality addressed should encompass an inclusive public policy front, for example material matters such as wealth, inequality and redistribution that are so much the stuff of politics and often treated as separate from the directly moral sphere. The alternative would be for the overview function to be confined to personal relations and life/death existential matters. This conundrum is left open for debate around questions of feasibility and pragmatism as the obstacles to getting the show on the road would undoubtedly be great and starting small may be the preferred, even only option.

Gnawing questions

Numerous questions gnaw as a consequence of the discussion's findings and conclusions. Key amongst these are whether we are on firmer ground as a consequence of scientific findings – or as much at sea as ever – and is that degree of uncertainty likely to be exacerbated by an endorsement of relativism?

Total watertight answers to dilemmas extant over centuries past would be a delusory expectation by any reckoning. What have emerged from this study, however, are insights and pointers, and these pointers are not just in the direction of a lack of definition or answers. Despite the reservations, there are some counterbalances to the uncertainties that need reiteration as the discussion closes.

The role of science

Notwithstanding the caveats that must be borne in mind in relation to science – the danger of being seduced by its kudos and of it being used to simply back up pre-conceptions – the evidence indicates that there have been scientific gains in understanding morality. The forensic detail in mapping the brain has diminished, even if it has not eliminated, the degree to which discourse is conducted in the shadows sustaining wished for beliefs and narratives. The revelations about the operation of the brain tell us about the nature of impulse and cognitive control systems. What they do not do, however, is provide comprehensive behavioural analysis or anticipate behaviour and its underlying thought processes because of the impact of culture, experience and the idiosyncrasies of the individual. That is not to say that science is precluded from making inroads in these areas, but they are outside the scope of certainty – black and white answers. Is this knowledge of the grounding of behaviour in its biological roots therefore of much use? The answer vouchsafed here is that it is. It offers insight into the biological foundation of behaviour and morality – and gives a clearer understanding of what can be expected in terms of modification. It provides the possibility of deliverance from the yoke of an unrealistic anticipation of progress; deliverance from a constant sense of failure that is the consequence of an aspiration based on a false premise. It will help in reconciling us to a morality and public policy aspiration of managing impulses rather than 'bettering' them.

These findings are by no means a panacea, but that said the intention in embarking on this study was one of improving the relationship between morality and public policy, and for that an understanding of the truth, as far as we know it, of the operation of impulses and their interplay with fluid culture is necessary. Keeping that knowledge to the fore and updated is essential if the avoidance tendencies of governments with which we have become so familiar are to be countered.

The challenge of relativism

And what of relativism? The coexistence of a universal set of impulses at the root of behaviour, but malleable to a degree in terms of motive, action and accommodation through cultural and material pressures, brings us to a major challenge for public policy. Is an acceptance of a relativist stance, however logical in respect of the derivation and development of morality, feasible for public policy operation or are the uncertainties too great? There can be no doubt that the proposition poses quandaries for governments.

The divide between faith and secular values presents government with repeat dilemmas as it seeks to accommodate respect for religious beliefs in the face of contradictory drives towards human fulfilment from the secular world. We have witnessed tensions in relation to medical ethics, sexuality and sexual behaviour, existential issues associated with birth and death – and more. The balancing act required of government in these matters is problematic and is undoubtedly a contributory factor to its avoidance tactics and less than adequate response in the moral sphere.

Governmental concerns over divergent values also relate to allegiance to the state – the fraught question of national identity. Anxieties over sustaining cohesion are evident in the British government's moves to reinforce a sense of citizenship through the education curriculum in schools (Department for Education, 2013), and in measures to counter the propagation of values at odds with national identity and equality commitments (BBC, 2014c; Garner, 2014). The Prevent Programme, seeking to contain the influences that lead to terrorist activity, is a further example of such attempts to shore up a shared value system in the context of an influential counter culture (HM Government, 2008; Gardner, 2015).

It would be fair to say that a complete public policy hands-off modus operandi would not be manageable in terms of holding a jurisdiction together. Some degree of cohesion is necessary in order to function. Perhaps the object should be to facilitate plurality and changes in morality as far as possible within the parameters of the universal applicability of the law. Talking from first principles, the expectation would be that the framing of that law should allow for maximum plurality within the circumscription of human rights preservation. The logic of human rights protection has been argued in detail in Chapter Five across matters such as discrimination and a host of protective needs in the face of the capacity of the group to oppress or fail to care for individuals and sections of society.

As ever, the lines are blurred, but relativism does have a place within public policy. A principle of minimising unnecessary interference, while adhering to protective standards is the concept being advocated here. It is an open-minded position that presupposes an operational model that anticipates cultural difference. And by that token, it is one that also anticipates moral change as cultures and material pressures mutate. An openness and responsiveness to this difference and change is what is sought.

New ideas happen

There is no misconception here that the process of change being advocated in this book would be easy but, reflecting on the danger of operating in denial, it appears that movement in the direction of acknowledging the ubiquitous nature of morality, its role in accommodating impulses and its various contributory sources is the preferred way forward. Finally, to stiffen the resolve – the institution of new ideas happens; it is not the stuff of dreams. Being daunted and shuffling away under the pretext of thinking 'it will never happen' would be an unnecessary self fulfilling prophecy. Changes in perception and how a society operates are integral to history, and most particularly they are the burden and blessing of the 20th and 21st centuries. It has been a period that has witnessed population movements consequent on war and hope, the decline of socialism, a reordering of the world map, a surge in both nationalism and internationalism and in global communication and information distribution on a scale and with a degree of potency inconceivable in the past. Change has several geneses; sometimes it is the upshot of vision and sometimes it happens inexorably under the pressure of circumstance, and sometimes it is consequent on both these scenarios. It can be incremental or sudden, or with elements of both modes as, for example, with the collapse of the Soviet empire. The explanation and certainty of any of these development patterns remain elusive; group behaviour and the wiring of thought across populations are unpredictable.

With such a degree of uncertainty it would be foolhardy to lay down a detailed prospectus for the proposals made in this discussion – certainly absurd to append a timetable. But the possibility of a shift in response to nudges and a host of influences is real and worthy of contemplation and debate. Furthermore, whatever view may be taken of the book's analysis of the nature of morality, few would dispute the need for governments to address the moral issues of the day from a position of optimum awareness and greater readiness to make a judgement about whether or not public policy change is needed. It is therefore worth emphasising that, if the will is there, the establishment of a resource to facilitate such an enhancement could be achieved within a relatively short space of time; a parliamentary session is all that is required.

References

Abse, L. (1966) 'Why should homosexuality be decriminalised?' interview on *The Today Programme*, BBC, 20 December (www.bbc.co.uk/archive/gay_rights/12005.shtml)

Adler, A. (1929) *The Practice and Theory of Individual Psychology*, translated by P. Radin, London: Routledge & Kegan Paul

Al-Ghazali, A. (2002) *The Incoherence of the Philosophers*, Chicago: University of Chicago Press

Aquinas, T. (1975) *Summa Contra Gentiles*, Chicago: University of Notre Dame Press

Aquinas, T. (2007) *Summa Theological*, Hayes Barton: Hayes Barton Press

Aristotle (2004) *Nicomachean Ethics*, H. Tredennick (ed), London: Penguin Classics

Arnold, M. (1867) *Dover Beach* (www.poetryfoundation.org/poem/172844)

Assmann, J. (2004) 'Monotheism and polytheism', in S. Iles Johnston (ed) *Religions of the Ancient World: A Guide*, pp 17–31, Cambridge, MA: Belknap Press

Auden, W. (1940) 'In memory of Sigmund Freud', in *Another Time*, London: Random House (www.poets.org/poetsorg/poem/memory-sigmund-freud)

Avakian, B. (2007) *Why Is Religious Fundamentalism Growing in Today's World—And what is the Real Alternative?* (www.revcom.us/a/104/avakian-religion-en.html)

Ayer, A. (1936) *Language, Truth and Logic*, London: Victor Gollancz Ltd

Barlow, A., Burgoyne, C., Clery, E. and Smithson, J. (2008) 'Cohabitation and the law: myths, money and the media', in A. Park, J. Curtice and K. Thomson (eds) *British Social Attitudes: The 24th Report*, pp 29–51, London: Sage Publications

Barlow, A., Duncan, S., James, G. and Park, A. (2001) 'Just a piece of paper? Marriage and cohabitation', in A. Park, J. Curtice and K. Thomson (eds) *British Social Attitudes: The 18th Report, Public Policy, Social Ties*, pp 29–57, London: Sage Publications

Bauer, M., Jordan, A., Green-Pedersen, C. and Heretier, A. (eds) (2012) *Dismantling Public Policy. Preferences, Strategies and Effects*, Oxford: Oxford University Press

Baumrind, D. (1967) 'Child care practices anteceding three patterns of pre-school behavior', *Genetic Psychology Monographs*, vol 75, pp 43–88

BBC (2009) 'Agencies obey gay adoption rules', *BBC News*, 1 January (http://news.bbc.co.uk/1/hi/uk/7806780.stm)

BBC (2011) 'David Cameron sets out Welfare Reform Bill plans' *BBC News Politics*, 17 February (www.bbc.co.uk/news/uk-politics-12486158)

BBC (2014a) 'Assisted dying: Desmond Tutu signals support', *BBC News UK*, 13 July (www.bbc.co.uk/news/uk-28282323)

BBC (2014b) 'Behind closed doors. Elderly care exposed', *Panorama*, BBC, 30 April (www.bbc.co.uk/programmes/b042rcjp)

BBC (2014c) 'How will government shut out the Trojan Horse?' *BBC News Education & Family*, 10 June (www.bbc.co.uk/news/education-27024881)

Bentham, J. (1780/2007) *Introduction to the Principles of Morals and Legislation*, New York: Dover

Berger P. (1992) *A far Glory: The Quest for Faith in the Age of Credulity*, New York: Free Press

Berlin, I. (1969) *Four essays on liberty*, Oxford: Oxford University Press

Beveridge, W. (1942) *Social Insurance and Allied Services* (www.nationalarchives.gov.uk/cabinetpapers/themes/beveridge-bevan)

British Humanist Association (2012) 'Holy redundant. Remove bishops from parliament', *BHA News*, issue 3/2012

British Humanist Association (2014a) organisation website (https://humanism.org.uk)

British Humanist Association (2014b) *Faith Schools* (https://humanism.org.uk/campaigns/schools-and-education/faith-schools/)

British Humanist Association (2015) *BHA Education Policy* (https://humanism.org.uk/education/education-policy/)

Bruce S. (2000) *Fundamentalism*, Malden, MA: Blackwell

Bynner, J. (2001) 'Childhood risks and protective factors in social exclusion'. *Children and Society*, vol 15(5), pp 285–301

Cameron, D. (2014) 'My faith in the Church of England', *Church Times*, 16 April (www.churchtimes.co.uk/articles/2014/17-april/comment/opinion/my-faith-in-the-church-of-england)

Chase-Lansdale, P. and Hetherington, E, (1990) 'The impact of divorce on lifespan developments: short and long term effects', in P. Baltes, D. Featherman and R. Lerner (eds) *Life Span Development and Behavior*, Hillsdale, NJ: Erlbaum Associates

Church of England (2014) *Assisted Suicide* (www.churchofengland.org/our-views/medical-ethics-health-social-care-policy/assisted-suicide.aspx)

Commission on Families and the Wellbeing of Children (2005) *Families and the state: Two-way Support and Responsibility*, Bristol: The Policy Press

Commission on Funding of Care and Support (2011) *Fairer care funding. The report of the Commission on Funding of Care and Support* (www.wp.dh.gov.uk/carecommission/)

Commission on Social Justice (1994) *Social Justice: Strategies for National Renewal*, London: Institute for Public Policy Research

Committee on Homosexual Offences and Prostitution (1957) *Report of the Committee on Homosexual Offences and Prostitution*, Home Office, The Scottish Home Department, London: Her Majesty's Stationery Office, reprinted 1963 as *The Wolfenden Report: Report of the Committee on Homosexual Offences and Prostitution*, New York: Stein and Day

Committee of Inquiry into Human Fertilisation and Embryology (1984) *Report of the Committee of Inquiry into Human Fertilisation and Embryology*, Department of Health and Social Security (www.hfea.gov.uk/docs/Warnock_Report_of_the_Committee_of_Inquiry_into_Human_Fertilisation_and_Embryology_1984.pdf)

ComRes (2010) 'Poll shows public support growing for assisted suicide', *Panorama*, BBC, 31 January (http://news.bbc.co.uk/panorama/hi/front_page/newsid_8487000/8487768.stm)

Conrad, P. (2013) 'The silence of animals by John Gray – review', *Guardian*, 3 March (www.theguardian.com/books/2013/mar/03/silence-animals-john-gray-review)

Conservative Party (2010) *The Conservative Manifesto. Invitation to Join the Government of Britain* (www.conservatives.com/~/media/files/activist%20centre/press%20and%20policy/manifestos/manifesto2010)

Crown Prosecution Service (2015) *Violence against Women and Girls* (www.cps.gov.uk/Publications/equality/vaw/)

Cupitt, D. (1984) *The Sea of Faith*, London: British Broadcasting Corporation

Darwin, C. (1859) *On the Origin of Species*, London: John Murray

Darwin, C. (1871) *The Descent of Man, and Selection in Relation to Sex*, 1981 facsimile of original edition, Princeton, New Jersey: Princeton University Press (https://teoriaevolutiva.files.wordpress.com/2014/02/darwin-c-the-descent-of-man-and-selection-in-relation-to-sex.pdf)

Dawkins, R. (1976) *The Selfish Gene*, Oxford: Oxford University Press

Dawkins, R. (1986) *The Blind Watchmaker*, New York: Norton & Company, Inc.

Dawkins, R. (2006) *The God Delusion*, New York: Bantam Books

Deech, Baroness (2010) *Sisters, there were never such devoted sisters*, Gresham College lecture, 2 February (www.gresham.ac.uk/lectures-and-events/sisters-sisters-there-were-never-such-devoted-sisters)

Department for Education (2013) *Statutory Guidance. National Curriculum in England: Citizenship Programmes of Study for Key Stages 3 and 4* (www.gov.uk/government/publications/national-curriculum-in-england-citizenship-programmes-of-study/national-curriculum-in-england-citizenship-programmes-of-study-for-key-stages-3-and-4)

Descartes, R. (1641) 'Meditations on first philosophy', in J. Cottingham (ed) (1996) *Meditations on First Philosophy with Selections from the Objections and Replies* (revised ed.), Cambridge: Cambridge University Press

Donnelly, J. (2003) *Universal Human Rights in Theory and Practice*, Ithaca, NY: Cornell University Press

Doris, J.M. (2002) *Lack of Character*, Cambridge: Cambridge University Press

Dorling, D. (2014) *Inequality and the 1%*, New York: Verso

Doward, J. (2015) 'One person a fortnight travels to Dignitas from Britain to end their lives', *Observer* 15 August (www.theguardian.com/society/2015/aug/15/assisted-dying-britons-dignitas-rises-campaigners-change-law)

Duncan, S. and Phillips, M. (2008) 'New families? Tradition and change in modern relationships', in A. Park, J. Curtice and K. Thomson (eds) *British Social Attitudes: The 24th Report*, pp 1–21, London: Sage Publications

Dworkin, R. (2013) *Religion without God*, Cambridge MA: Harvard University Press

Eagleton, T. (2001) 'Marx' in R. Monk and F. Raphael (eds) *The Great Philosophers. From Socrates to Turing*, pp 265–306, London: Phoenix

The Economist (2008) 'Working mothers, unite!', 10 July (www.economist.com/node/11708457)

Elliot, L. and Pilkington, E. (2015) 'New Oxfam report says half global wealth held by the 1%', *Guardian*, 19 January (www.theguardian.com/business/2015/jan/19/global-wealth-oxfam-inequality-davos-economic-summit-switzerland)

Emerson, M. and Hartman, D. (2006) 'The rise of religious fundamentalism', *Annual Review Sociology 2006*, vol 32, pp 127–44

Equality and Human Rights Commission (2011) *Close to Home: An Inquiry into Older People and Human Rights in Home Care* (www. equalityhumanrights.com/legal-and-policy/our-legal-work/ inquiries-and-assessments/inquiry-home-care-older-people/ download-inquiry-report)

Equality and Human Rights Commission (2015) *Description of the Equality and Human Rights Commission's Function and Operation* (www. equalityhumanrights.com/about-us)

Esping-Andersen, G. (1990) *The Three Worlds of Welfare Capitalism*, Cambridge: Polity Press

Esping-Andersen, G. (1999) *Social Foundations of Postindustrial Economies*, Oxford: Oxford University Press

Eurobarometer (2005) *Social Values, Science and Technology* (http:// ec.europa.eu/public_opinion/archives/ebs/ebs_225_report_en.pdf)

European Union (2014) *Sweden: Sweden: Successful Reconciliation of Work and Family Life* (http://europa.eu/epic/countries/sweden/ index_en.htm)

Eurostat (2011) *Children at Risk of Poverty or Social Exclusion*, European Commission (http://ec.europa.eu/eurostat/statistics-explained/ index.php/Children_at_risk_of_poverty_or_social_exclusion)

Fagan, A. (2015) 'Human rights', *The Internet Encyclopedia of Philosophy*, ISSN 2161–0002 (www.iep.utm.edu/hum-rts/#H1)

Fairbairn, C. (2014) '"Common law marriage" and cohabitation', *House of Commons Library Standard Note SN03372* (www.parliament. uk/business/publications/research/briefing-papers/SN03372/ common-law-marriage-and-cohabitation)

Faith Leaders (2014) 'Assisted dying bill: faith leaders statement', *Telegraph*, 16 July (www.telegraph.co.uk/news/religion/10970955/ Assisted-dying-bill-faith-leaders-statement.html)

Fontes, L. and McCloskey, K. (2011) 'Cultural issues in violence against women', in C. Renzetti, J. Edleson and R. Bergen (eds) *Sourcebook on Violence against Women* (2nd ed.), pp 151–169, Thousand Oaks, CA: Sage

Freud, S. (1905) *On Sexuality: Three Essays on the Theory of Sexuality and Other Works*, A. Richards (ed) (1991), London: Penguin

Freud, S. (1920) *Beyond the Pleasure Principle*, translated by C. J. M. Hubback, London, Vienna: International Psycho-Analytical, 1922; Bartleby.com, 2010 (www.bartleby.com/276/)

Fuster, J., Bodner, M. and Kroger, J. (2000) 'Cross-modal and cross-temporal association in neurons of frontal cortex', *Nature*, 405 (6784), pp 347–51

Gardner, F. (2015) 'Prevent strategy: Is it failing to stop radicalisation?', *BBC News*, 6 March (www.bbc.co.uk/news/uk-31756755)

Garner, R. (2014) 'Islamist school scandal: Head teachers have fears religious leaders are influencing schools across country', *Independent*, 2 May (www.independent.co.uk/news/education/education-news/islamist-school-scandal-head-teachers-have-fears-religious-leaders-are-influencing-schools-across-country-9318368.html)

Gerard, J. and Buehler, C. (2004) 'Cumulative environmental risk and youth maladjustment: The role of youth attributes', *Child Development*, vol 75(6), pp 1832–49

Gray, J. (2013) *The Silence of Animals: On Progress and Other Modern Myths*, New York: Farrar, Straus and Giroux

Gray, J. (2014) 'Moral tribes: emotion, reason and the gap between us and them by Joshua Greene – review', *Guardian*, 17 January (www.theguardian.com/books/2014/jan/17/moral-tribes-joshua-greene-review)

Grayling, A. (2004) *The Mystery of Things*, London: Weidenfeld & Nicholson

Greene, J. (2003) 'From neural 'is' to moral 'ought': what are the moral implications of neuroscientific moral psychology?', *Nature Reviews Neuroscience*, vol 4, pp 847–50

Greene, J. (2014) *Moral Tribes: Emotion, Reason and the Gap between Us and Them*, London: Atlantic

Haidt, J. (2001) 'The emotional dog and its rational tail: A social intuitionist approach to moral judgment,' *Psychological Review*, vol 108, pp 814–34

Haidt, J. (2007) 'The new synthesis in moral psychology,' *Science*, vol 316, pp 998–1002

Haidt, J. (2012) *The Righteous Mind. Why Good People are Divided*, London: Allen Lane

Hamilton, C. (2008) *The Freedom Paradox: Towards a Post-Secular Ethics*, Sydney: Allen & Unwin

Harman, G. (1999) 'Moral philosophy meets social psychology: Virtue ethics and the fundamental attribution error,' *Proceedings of the Aristotelian Society*, vol 99, pp 315–31

Hauser, M. (2006) *Moral Minds: How Nature Designed our Universal Sense of Right and Wrong*, New York: Ecco/Harper Collins Publishers

Heard, A. (1997) *Human Rights: Chimeras in Sheep's Clothing?* (www.sfu.ca/~aheard/intro.html)

Henricson, C. (2007) *The Contractual Culture and Family Services: A Discussion*, London: Family and Parenting Institute

Henricson, C. (2012) *A Revolution in Family Policy. Where we should go from here*, Bristol: Policy Press

Henricson, C. and Bainham, A. (2005) *The Child and Family Policy Divide*, York: Joseph Rowntree Foundation

HM Government (2008) *The Prevent Strategy. A Guide for Local Partners in England. Stopping People Becoming or Supporting Terrorists and Violent Extremists* (http://resources.cohesioninstitute.org.uk/Publications/Documents/Document/Default.aspx?recordId=134)

Hobbes, T. (1651) *Leviathan*, C. MacPherson (ed) (1981), London: Penguin Classics

Holloway, R. (2009) *Between the Monster and the Saint*, Edinburgh: Canongate Books

Hope, C. (2010) 'Equality watchdog spent £1 million making staff redundant and rehiring them, MPs say', *Telegraph*, 4 March (www.telegraph.co.uk/news/politics/7360317/Equality-watchdog-spent-1million-making-staff-redundant-and-rehiring-them-MPs-say.html)

Hume, D. (1738/1888) *A Treatise of Human Nature*, Oxford: Clarendon Press

Hunt, S. (ed) (2009) *Family Trends: British Families since the 1950s*, London: Family and Parenting Institute

Huxley, A. (1932) *Brave New World*, London: Chatto & Windus

Jago, M. (2014) *Clement Attlee: The Inevitable Prime Minister*, London: Biteback

Jha, A. (2006) 'Peter Higgs criticises Richard Dawkins over anti-religious 'fundamentalism'', *Guardian*, 26 December (www.theguardian.com/science/2012/dec/26/peter-higgs-richard-dawkins-fundamentalism)

Jones, E., Gutman, L. and Platt, L. (2013) *Family Stressors and Children's Outcomes*, London: Department for Education (www.gov.uk/government/uploads/system/uploads/attachment_data/file/219639/DFE-RR254.pdf)

Kant, I. (1785/2005) *Groundwork of the Metaphysic of Morals*, London and New York: Routledge Classics

Kellert, S. (1993) *In the wake of chaos*, Chicago: University of Chicago Press

Labour Party (1997) *New Labour because Britain deserves Better* (www.politicsresources.net/area/uk/man/lab97.htm)

Lagarde, C. (2014) *Economic Inclusion and Financial Integrity—an Address to the Conference on Inclusive Capitalism*, London, 27 May (www.imf.org/external/np/speeches/2014/052714.htm)

Laming, Lord (2003) *The Victoria Climbié Report*, London: The Stationery Office

Laming, Lord (2009) *The Protection of Children in England: A Progress Report*, London: The Stationery Office

Law Commission (2011) *Adult Social Care*, London: The Stationery Office

Law Commission (2015) *Description of the Law Commission's Function and Operation* (http://lawcommission.justice.gov.uk/about-us.htm)

Lawrence, D. (1913) *Sons and Lovers*, C. Baron and H. Baron (eds) (1992), Cambridge: Cambridge University Press

Lawrence, D. (1920) *Women in Love*, D. Farmer, L. Vasey and J. Worthen (eds) (1987), Cambridge: Cambridge University Press

Lawrence, D. (1928) *Lady Chatterley's Lover*, M. Squires (ed) (1993), Cambridge: Cambridge University Press

Leibniz, G. (1710) *Theodicy: Essays on the Goodness of God, the Freedom of Man, and the Origin of Evil*, translated by E. Huggard, edited by A. Farrer (1951), Chicago/La Salle: Open Court

Leigh, M. (2004) *Vera*, S. Williams (producer), UK: Momentum Pictures

Levenstein, M. (2013) 'A third way', *Royal Society of Arts Journal*, issue 2013 (4)

Leveson, the Right Honourable Lord Justice (2012) *An Inquiry into the Culture, Practices and Ethics of the Press* (http://webarchive.nationalarchives.gov.uk/20140122145147/http://www.official-documents.gov.uk/document/hc1213/hc07/0780/0780_ii.pdf)

Lipscombe, S. and Barber, S. (2014) 'Assisted suicide', *House of Commons Library Standard Note SN/HA/4857* (http://researchbriefings.files.parliament.uk/documents/SN04857/SN04857.pdf)

Liptak, A. (2008) 'Inmate count in U.S. dwarfs other nations', *New York Times* 23 April (www.nytimes.com/2008/04/23/us/23prison.html?pagewanted=all&_r=0)

Locke, J. (1690) *Second Treatise on Government* (www.gutenberg.org/files/7370/7370-h/7370-h.htm)

Malik, K. (2014) *The Quest for a Moral Compass. A Global History of Ethics*, London: Atlantic Books

Marx, K. and Engels, F. (1845–46/1974) *The German Ideology*, London: Lawrence & Wishart

Marx, K. and Engels, F. (1859/1968) *Selected Works*, London: Lawrence & Wishart

Marx, K. and Engels, F. (1975/2005) *The Collected Works of Karl Marx and Frederick Engels*, London: Lawrence & Wishart

McCarthy, A. (2014) 'The shallow nihilism of John Gray', *Spiked Review of Books*, 10 October (www.spiked-online.com/review_of_books/article/the-shallow-nihilism-of-john-gray/15999#.VQPwUBymvQU)

McEwan, I. (2014) *The Children Act*, London: Jonathan Cape

McGrath, A. and McGrath, J. (2007) *Dawkins Delusion*, London: Society for Promoting Christian Knowledge (SPCK)

Micklethwait, J. and Wooldridge, A. (2010) *God is Back. How the Global Rise of Faith is Changing the World*, London: Penguin Books

Midgley, M. (1984) *Wickedness*, London: Routledge

Midgley, M. (2014) *Are you an Illusion?*, London: Routledge

Mill, J. (1859) *On Liberty* (2nd ed.), London: John W. Parker & Son.

Mill, J. (1863) *Utilitarianism*, London: Parker, Son, and Bourn, p 14 (https://archive.org/stream/a592840000milluoft#page/14/mode/2up)

Mill, J. (1863/1992) *On Liberty and Utilitarianism*, Everyman's Library, London: David Campbell's Publishers

Miller, E., Freedman, D. and Wallis, J. (2002) 'The prefrontal cortex: categories, concepts and cognition', *Philosophical Transactions of the Royal Society of London. Series B, Biological Sciences*, 357 (1424), pp 1123–36

Moll, J. and de Oliveira-Souze, R. (2007) 'Moral judgements, emotions and the utilitarian brain', *Trends in Cognitive Sciences*, vol 11(8), pp 319–21

Munro, E. (2011) *The Munro Review of Child Protection: Final Report* (www.gov.uk/government/collections/munro-review)

NatCen (2013) *Trust, Politics and Institutions* (www.bsa.natcen.ac.uk/latest-report/british-social-attitudes-30/key-findings/trust-politics-and-institutions.aspx)

NatCen (2014) *British Social Attitudes Survey – Morality* (www.bsa-data.natcen.ac.uk)

National Assembly of France (1789) *Declaration of the Rights of Man and the Citizen* (www.conseil-constitutionnel.fr/conseil-constitutionnel/root/bank_mm/anglais/cst2.pdf)

Nice, G. (2014) *Human Rights: Philosophy and History*, speech at Gresham College, 15 October (www.gresham.ac.uk/lectures-and-events/human-rights-philosophy-and-history)

Nickel, J. (1992) 'Human rights', in L. Becker and C. Becker (eds), *Encyclopedia of Ethics*, London: St. James Press, pp 561–65

Nietzsche, F (1886) *Beyond Good and Evil*, translated by R. Hollingdale (2003), London: Penguin Classics

Observer (2015) 'Humanism has a place in religious education', *Observer*, 8 February

Office for National Statistics (2005) *National Statistics. Focus on Ethnicity and Identity* (2001 census) (www.ons.gov.uk/ons/rel/ethnicity/focus-on-ethnicity-and-identity/focus-on-ethnicity-and-identity-summary-report/index.html)

Office of the Children's Commissioner (2013) *"If only someone had listened": Office of the Children's Commissioner's Inquiry into Child Sexual Exploitation in Gangs and Groups final report*, London: Office of the Children's Commissioner

Otto, R. (1958) *The Idea of the Holy*, translated by John W. Harvey. London: Oxford University Press

Owen, M. (2014) 'UK: indifference to ending discrimination against women', *Open Democracy*, 20 October (www.opendemocracy.net/5050/margaret-owen/uk-indifference-to-ending-discrimination-against-women)

Owen, J. (2015) 'Bishops 'should make way for other faiths in Lords'', *Independent*, 7 December

Paine, T. (1791) *Rights of Man*, London: J.S. Jordan

Pegram, T. (2011) *The Equality and Human Rights Commission Challenges and Opportunities*, London: Artas and Humanities Research Council (www.ahrc.ac.uk/documents/project-reports-and-reviews/ahrc-public-policy-series/the-equality-and-human-rights-commission-challenges-and-opportunites/)

Pew Research Center. Religion and Public Life (2006) *Spirit and Power: A 10-Country Survey of Pentecostals* (www.pewforum.org/2006/10/05/spirit-and-power/)

Pew Research Center. Religion & Public Life (2012) *The Global Religious Landscape* (www.pewforum.org/2012/12/18/global-religious-landscape-exec/)

Philp, M. (2013) 'Thomas Paine' in E. Zalta (ed) *The Stanford Encyclopedia of Philosophy* (Winter 2013 edition) (http://plato.stanford.edu/archives/win2013/entries/paine)

Pierson, P. (1994) *Dismantling the Welfare State: Reagan, Thatcher and the Politics of Retrenchment*, Cambridge: Cambridge University Press

Piketty, T. (2014) *Capital in the Twenty-First Century*, Cambridge, MA: Harvard University Press

Pinker, S. (2012) *The Better Angels of our Nature. A History of Violence and Humanity*, London: Penguin (First published in Great Britain by Allen Lane)

Pope Paul VI (1968) *Encyclical letter humanae vitae of the supreme pontiff Paul VI to his venerable brothers the patriarchs, archbishops, bishops and other local ordinaries in peace and communion with the apostolic see, to the clergy and faithful of the whole catholic world, and to all men of good will, on the regulation of birth* (http://w2.vatican.va/content/paul-vi/en/encyclicals/documents/hf_p-vi_enc_25071968_humanae-vitae.html)

Rawls, J. (1971) *A Theory of Justice*, Cambridge, MA: Harvard University Press

Rhodes, J. (2012) 'Outrage at Jimmy Savile conceals the fact that our culture encourages paedophilia. Believe me, I know what I'm talking about', *Telegraph*, 1 November (http://blogs.telegraph.co.uk/culture/jamesrhodes/100067072/outrage-at-jimmy-savile-conceals-the-fact-that-our-culture-encourages-paedophilia-believe-me-i-know-what-im-talking-about)

Richards, M. (1993) 'Learning from divorce', in C. Clulow (ed) *Does marriage matter?*, London: Karmac Books

Rose, N. and Abi-Rached, J. (2013) *Neuro: The New Brain Sciences and the Management of the Mind*, Princeton: Princeton University Press

Ross, T. and Bingham, J. (2012) 'MPs 'will not be forced to support gay marriage'', *Telegraph*, 14 March (www.telegraph.co.uk/news/politics/9144282/MPs-will-not-be-forced-to-support-gay-marriage.html)

Ruggiero, T. (2002) *Plato and the Theory of Forms*, Philosophical Society (www.philosophicalsociety.com/archives/plato%20and%20the%20theory%20of%20forms.htm)

Russell, B. (1930/2006) *The Conquest of Happiness*, London and New York: Routledge Classics

Sample, I. (2015) 'Three-parent babies explained: What are the concerns and are they justified', *Guardian*, 2 February (www.theguardian.com/science/2015/feb/02/three-parent-babies-explained)

Sartre, J. (1944) 'No exit' in *No Exit and Three Other Plays* (1989), London: Vintage

Schopenhauer, A. (1837) *On the Basis of Morality*, translated by E. Payne; introduction by D. Cartwright (1995), Providence: Berghahn Books

Sen, A. (1992) *Inequality Reexamined*, Cambridge, MA: Harvard University Press

Shestack, J. (1998) 'The philosophic foundations of human rights', *Human Rights Quarterly*, vol 20, no 2, pp 201–34

Shimamura, A. (2000) 'The role of the prefrontal cortex in dynamic filtering', *Psychobiology*, vol 28, pp 207–18

Singer, T., and Lamm, C. (2009) 'The social neuroscience of empathy', *The Year in Cognitive Neuroscience 2009: Annals of the New York Academy of Sciences*, 1156, pp 81–96

Smith, D. (2007) 'Believe it or not: the sceptics beat God in bestseller battle', *Guardian*, 12 August (www.theguardian.com/uk/2007/aug/12/religion.books)

Strawson, P. (1974) 'Social morality and individual ideal' in P. Strawson, *Freedom and Resentment and Other Essays*, London: Methuen

Sundström, G., Malmberg, B., Sancho Castiello, M., del Barrio, É., Castejon, P., Tortosa, M. and Johansson, L. (2008) 'Family care for elders in Europe: policies and practices' in M. Szinovacz and A. Davey (eds) *Caregiving Contexts: Cultural, Familial and Societal Implications*, pp 235–67, New York: Springer

Telegraph (2012) 'Waterhouse Inquiry: recommendations and conclusions', 6 November (www.telegraph.co.uk/news/uknews/crime/9657836/Waterhouse-Inquiry-recommendations-and-conclusions.html)

Telegraph (2014) 'David Cameron fosters division by calling Britain a 'Christian country', 20 April (www.telegraph.co.uk/comment/letters/10777417/David-Cameron-fosters-division-by-calling-Britain-a-Christian-country.html)

The Levin Institute, The State University of New York (2015) *Origins of Human Rights* (www.globalization101.org/uploads/File/HumanRights/humanrights.pdf)

Tribunal of Inquiry into the Abuse of Children in Care in the Former County Council Areas of Gwynedd and Clwyd since 1974 (2000) *Lost in Care* (http://tna.europarchive.org/20040216040105/http:/www.doh.gov.uk/lostincare/20102a.htm)

Tuschman, A. (2013) *Our Political Nature: The Evolutionary Origins of What Divides Us*, New York: Prometheus Books

United Nations General Assembly (1948) *Universal Declaration of Human Rights* (www.un.org/en/documents/udhr/)

United States Congress (1776) *United States Declaration of Human Rights* (www.archives.gov/exhibits/charters/declaration_transcript.html)

Werndl, C. (2009) 'What are the new implications of chaos for unpredictability?' *British Journal for the Philosophy of Science*, vol 60 (1): pp 195–220

Wilkinson, R. and Marmot, M. (2003) *Social Determinants of Health: The Solid Facts* (2nd ed.), Copenhagen: World Health Organisation (www.euro.who.int/__data/assets/pdf_file/0005/98438/e81384.pdf)

Williams, B. (1981) *Moral Luck*, Cambridge: Cambridge University Press

Wollny, I., Apps, J. and Henricson, C. (2010) *Can Government Measure Family Wellbeing?*, London: Family and Parenting Institute

Yellen, J. (2014) *Perspectives on Inequality and Opportunity from the Survey of Consumer Finances*, speech at the Conference on Economic Opportunity and Inequality, Federal Reserve Bank of Boston, Boston, MA, 17 October (www.federalreserve.gov/newsevents/speech/yellen20141017a.html)

Zaki, J., and Ochsner, K. (2012) 'The neuroscience of empathy: progress, pitfalls and promise', *Nature Neuroscience*, vol 15, pp 675–80

Index